COLLECTOR'S
COMPASS™

Barbie®
DOLL

Martingale
& C O M P A N Y

Bothell, Washington

Credits

President . . . . Nancy J. Martin
CEO . . . . Daniel J. Martin
Publisher . . . . Jane Hamada
Editorial Director . . . . Mary V. Green
Editorial Project Manager . . . . .Tina Cook
Series Editor . . . . Christopher J. Kuppig
Design and Production Manager . . . . Stan Green
Series Designer . . . . Bonnie Mather
Production Designer . . . . Jennifer LaRock Shontz
Series Concept . . . . Michael O. Campbell

Collector's Compass™: Barbie® Doll
© 2000 by Martingale & Company

Martingale & Company
PO Box 118
Bothell, WA 98041-0118 USA
www.martingale-pub.com

Printed in Canada
05 04 03 02 01 00 6 5 4 3 2 1

Library of Congress Cataloging-in-Publication Data
Collector's Compass: Barbie doll
　　p. cm. — (Collector's compass)
　　ISBN 1-56477-343-4
　　1. Barbie dolls—Collectors and collecting. I. Series
NK4894.3.B37 B3745 2000
688.7'221—dc21   00-042372

Mission Statement

We are dedicated to providing quality products and service by working
together to inspire creativity and to enrich the lives we touch.

CONTENTS

FOREWORD

As America's favorite hobby, collecting is exciting, gratifying, and above all, fun—but without the right knowledge, you could be destined for disappointment. Luckily, you've just found the most resourceful and inspiring series of guidebooks available to help you learn more about collecting. The *Collector's Compass*™ series approaches collecting in a whole new way, making it easy to learn about your favorite collectible categories—from the basics to the best-kept secrets.

The International Society of Appraisers (ISA) is pleased to be associated with the *Collector's Compass*™ series. As the ISA celebrates twenty years of professional education and certification of personal property appraisers, who currently specialize in over two hundred areas of expertise, we remain committed to setting the highest standards for our accredited members. The *Collector's Compass*™ series of reference books reflects the ISA's dedication to quality and integrity.

Christian Coleman, ISA CAPP, Ret.
Executive Director, International Society of Appraisers

INTRODUCTION

Whether it means setting the alarm clock for Saturday morning yard sales, watching "Antiques Roadshow," or chasing down childhood memories on eBay, collecting has become America's favorite hobby. The joy of finding treasure amid the clutter of a tag sale or a screen full of online offerings is infectious. Who could resist a pastime that combines the fun of shopping, the thrill of the hunt, the lure of a bargain, and the pride of ownership?

Throngs of novice collectors are joining experienced veterans in online bidding and weekend "antiquing" expeditions. If you count yourself among them, this book is for you.

The editors of *Collector's Compass* realized that today's collectors needed more information than was available, in an accessible and convenient format. Going beyond available price and identification guides, *Collector's Compass* books introduce the history behind a particular collectible, the fascinating aspects that make it special, and exclusive tips on where and how to search for exciting pieces.

Furthermore, the *Collector's Compass* series is uniquely reliable. Each volume is created by a carefully chosen team of dealers, appraisers, and other experts. Their collaboration ensures that each title will contain accurate and current information, as well as the secrets they've learned in a lifetime of collecting.

We hope that in the *Collector's Compass* series we have addressed every area essential to building a collection. Whether you're a newcomer or an experienced collector, we're sure this series will lead you to new treasures. Enjoy the adventure!

COLLECTING BARBIE® DOLLS

The Barbie® Doll as a Collectible

There are probably as many reasons that people collect Barbie® dolls as there are Barbie® dolls themselves. But in the most general terms, people collect Barbie® dolls as an expression of themselves, their interests, and their most cherished wishes and desires.

The Barbie® doll and her accessories offer collectors a sense of pure perfection, a perfection that only miniaturization can make possible. And the Barbie® doll fantasy combines the beauty of glamorous fashions, the fun of role-playing, and an ideal of the feminine form that still provokes comment more than forty years after the first Barbie® doll emerged.

Childhood fantasies in which Barbie® dolls played a starring role frequently spark the desire to start collecting. From the beloved doll that's gone missing over the years to that particular doll that was often wished for but never owned, the opportunity to recapture and rekindle the childhood memories that Barbie® dolls represent has been the inspiration behind many a collection.

For other collectors, the Barbie® doll and her luxurious wardrobe add a splash of excitement to the predictability of life in the full-sized world. Their closets may not be filled with

opposite:
Ponytail
Barbie® doll
in Roman
Holiday

7

fur-trimmed brocade suits, glittering ball gowns, or costumes of fabulous workmanship, but they can still revel in such treasures—even if only on a miniature scale—by collecting the Barbie® doll.

Finally, there are collectors who decide to invest in the Barbie® doll, hoping that they will be able to sell their collections later for a profit. They study the literature, become versed in the rarity of particular dolls, and try to snap up dolls they think will appreciate in value or add prestige to their collection.

The Special Allure of Barbie® Dolls

Every collectible category has its own history, even its own legends—but when it comes to the Barbie® doll, there is something very special about buying, selling, and owning. Mothers buy them for their daughters, grandmothers buy them for their grandchildren, and countless others buy just for themselves. The Barbie® dolls that collectors choose to purchase often reflect their personality—just go to any toy store and watch a shopper lose track of time as she compares Barbie® dolls back and forth before making a final decision about which one to take home!

Over the years, collecting Barbie® dolls has evolved into a very personal pastime—and sometimes it's more than the dolls themselves that creates the most excitement for collectors. *Why* people collect Barbie® dolls and *how* they go about building their collections are both part of the fun. The passion people feel about collecting Barbie® dolls can't be measured by quantity or value alone. Those with extensive collections are sometimes less excited about their dolls than collectors with only a doll or two. Someone who spends less than twenty-five dollars a month on her collection may place more significance on her Barbie® doll purchase than someone who regularly spends thousands of dollars on Barbie® doll items. Perhaps this passion is something you've already felt—the exhilaration of finding a Vintage doll in perfect condition, or the thrill of finally locating a doll after months of searching. It's all part of the joy of collecting Barbie® dolls.

But if there's one thing that all collectors have in common, it's that once you fall in love with Barbie® doll collecting, it's hard to stop—and even more difficult to part with any of your dolls. In

opposite:
1964 Bubble Cut Barbie® doll in Candy Striper

fact, it's common for Barbie® doll collectors never to sell their collections during their lifetimes, leaving family members to manage their collections after they've passed away. If collectors do sell, it's usually reluctantly, and often due to space or financial constraints. Even then, they can't easily resist the appeal of the doll. Chances are that they'll still buy the collector magazines and browse the Barbie® doll section of the toy stores. Soon enough, many begin collecting again.

The Two Eras of Collectible Barbie® Dolls

There are two distinct periods of production in the Barbie® doll collecting world: "Vintage," referring to dolls manufactured from 1959 to 1972; and "Contemporary," which generally refers to the period from the late 1980s to the present day. Mattel went through a period of financial hardship during the 1970s that adversely impacted the quality of its products. Collectors typically aren't interested in dolls manufactured during this period.

Mattel's rebirth in the 1980s was fueled in part by its recognition of the growing collectible market for Barbie® dolls. New themed Barbie® dolls, special series, designer editions, and other exclusive dolls and sets created an immediate demand for Barbie® dolls as a collectible. In their most valuable form, these dolls were never to leave their boxes. Of course, little girls still play with Barbie® dolls—even some of the higher-priced editions—but adult collectors usually prefer that Contemporary Barbie® dolls never be touched by human hands (other than by the hands at the Mattel factory).

Ponytail Barbie® doll in the classic striped bathing suit

In terms of value, there seems to be a recurring cycle. When Contemporary dolls are considered a "hot" collectible, Vintage languishes. Then Vintage comes back to life in the market and the new-issue Contemporary dolls are ignored. Barbie® doll experts believe that this seesaw of interest will continue, assuring that both segments of the market will retain long-term value and viability.

> **Did You Know?**
> Dolls are one of the most popular collectibles, second only to stamps.

The Barbie® Doll Collector

Although women in their forties and fifties most likely make up the largest segment of today's Barbie® doll–collecting population, people of all ages and both sexes enjoy collecting Barbie® dolls. In the late 1990s, Mattel stated that there were over 200,000 collectors in the United States alone. But an exact number, or even a good estimate, is hard to establish. Numbers can be gleaned from magazine subscriptions and club memberships, but not all collectors subscribe to the magazines on collecting Barbie® dolls and not all of them—probably not even the majority of them—belong to the Barbie® doll collectors' clubs.

There are countless ways to satisfy the Barbie® doll collecting bug. Some people collect only the Barbie® dolls they owned as children, while others collect dolls from a particular era. Some collect the Barbie® doll herself, while others collect a member of her family, such as the Skipper doll. Some people stick to collecting themed dolls, while some focus on collecting the vehicles, furniture, or other structures sold as accessories to the Barbie® doll. And of course, there are always those collectors whose goal is to simply build a glorious collection containing thousands of dolls!

The Barbie® doll's versatility makes her especially satisfying to collect. While the Vintage segment of the market makes the hunt and acquisition of a particular doll challenging for the experienced collector, the Contemporary market is open and easy to navigate for the newcomer. Even if a collector becomes discouraged with the pursuit of a particular piece, she can easily switch to another segment of the collectible category. Also appealing is the fact that prices for Barbie® dolls range from about $5 on up to $9,000, so

---

Till Death Do Us Part

One collector's estate featured several rare Barbie® dolls, purchased in 1959 and 1960. As much as the collector treasured them, to her dismay these early dolls didn't have bendable arms and legs that would allow her to pose them in seated positions. She remedied this "design flaw" by heating the dolls in an oven in order to soften their joints and bend their arms and legs. Her children remember coming home from school to be welcomed not by the aroma of cookies baking, but rather by the smell of Barbie® doll vinyl melting!

While the value of the dolls was destroyed, their outfits survived. The collector had carefully packed all of the extensive wardrobes she had purchased and they were all in perfect condition. Attendees of the estate sale had plenty to choose from and nearly everyone went home happy.

---

there's truly a doll out there for everyone—no matter the size of your pocketbook.

Collectors who fancy Vintage Barbie® dolls typically collect what fits their price range. In the early years, almost anyone could collect Vintage Barbie® dolls. But as interest has grown and values have increased, many people have switched to collecting less expensive dolls from the era, such as Ideal's Tammy and Topper's Dawn dolls.

The Contemporary era was sparked by the release of the 1988 Happy Holidays Barbie® doll. For many veteran collectors, it quickly became easier and less expensive to buy new Barbie® dolls. For a mere $15 to $50, a new doll could be added to a collection. And because of the quantity of dolls made, collectors were assured of getting the doll they wanted. Contemporary Barbie® doll collectors usually focus on series, such as the Happy Holidays Series and the International/Dolls of the World Collection, which was launched in 1980. Another favorite of Contemporary collectors is the Vintage Reproduction series, a series of vintage Barbie® doll reproductions. Porcelain and Bob Mackie Barbie® dolls are priced at the higher end of the spectrum, ranging from $150 to $900 per doll. Some department stores also have their own exclusive editions, which many Contemporary enthusiasts enjoy collecting.

Contemporary Barbie® doll collectors don't often switch to collecting Vintage Barbie® dolls, because reasonable prices and easy access to new dolls define the Contemporary collecting style. However, advanced Contemporary collectors who have collected all of the major series or who feel that they've gone as far as they want to go in collecting Contemporary Barbie® dolls may wish to revitalize their collecting interest by trying something different.

Mattel releases around two hundred or more dolls every year, so it doesn't take long to build a sizable Contemporary collection containing a few hundred dolls. In fact, Barbie® doll collections can become very big, very fast, sometimes incorporating thousands upon thousands of dolls over the years. Just trying to collect one of each Barbie® doll released in the United States drives the number up to about 2,700. Just imagine collecting every variation of hair, lip-paint color, or some other distinctive characteristic—the number can increase at an astonishing rate!

A Brief History of Barbie® Doll Collecting

As a collectible category, the Barbie® doll is just entering the "middle age" of a collectible's life cycle. The first generation of Barbie® doll collectors were essentially buying back their childhood. Collectors of the 1970s purchased dolls produced in the early 1960s.

Barbie® doll collecting remained fairly informal for several years. But eventually collectors started forming clubs and hosting conventions. Several price guides were published, some of which are still in print and regularly updated today. In 1988, Barbie® doll collecting became firmly established as a respected collectible category when a new concept surfaced: a magazine directed at the

Barbie® doll collector—*Barbie® Bazaar.* Soon the Barbie® doll–collecting trend began to snowball. By the early 1990s, both Vintage and Contemporary Barbie® doll collecting had become an exhilarating and challenging quest to find the next "rare" item.

By 1990, several monthly doll publications had hit the market. Suddenly it became easy for collectors to advertise items they wanted to sell or buy. Because such a large number of outfits and accessories play an important part of many Barbie® doll collections, collectors started advertising their "want" lists as well as their "for sale" lists. Buyers and sellers were connecting on a first-come, first-served basis. It wasn't unusual for the choice collectibles to be sold before a seller's list had even been widely mailed to the parties requesting it.

> **Did You Know?**
> The full name of the Barbie® doll is Barbara Millicent Roberts. According to legend, she hails from Willows, Wisconsin.

Value and Price Trends

Many factors determine the value of a Barbie® doll. By far, the most expensive Barbie® dolls to collect are the rarest Vintage Barbie® dolls—especially dolls that have never been played with and remain in like-new condition. Over the years, the prices of these older dolls increased so quickly that new collectors to the Barbie® doll market were discouraged because they could not even find, much less afford the Vintage items.

By the 1980s, Mattel had taken note of the escalating prices in the secondary market for its early Barbie® dolls, which had become more and more scarce as collectors sought them out. In response, Mattel produced a line of Special Edition Barbie® dolls intended to appeal directly to the collectible market. The first of these was the Happy Holidays Barbie® doll released in 1988. It was well received, and thus the era of Contemporary Barbie dolls began, with more Special Edition dolls being released each year since.

About ten years ago, the sheer enormity of the secondary-market supply of Barbie® dolls finally impacted their value. Consider this: from 1959 to 1988, total sales of the Barbie® doll exceeded 470 million. And up through 1987, nearly *one billion* Barbie® doll outfits were sold. That's a lot of Barbie® doll items for even the most massive and ravenous collecting audience!

Today, the Barbie® doll and her accessories are fairly well-established collectibles that have stabilized in value since the first wave of Barbie® doll collecting in the early 1970s. Common Vintage items have not increased much in value since 1992. This is attributed to a drop in the number of collectors who feel nostalgic for the early dolls and clothes, after a peak in the early 1990s.

Some Baby Boomers who collected Barbie® dolls in the 1970s and 1980s have now sold their collections or stored them away for their grandchildren. Prices for out-of-the-box, played-with items have declined in recent years due to reduced demand. However, prices for rare Vintage items have continued to climb. Because the market for early Barbie® doll items has diminished to some extent, many Vintage dealers have started catering more to the Contemporary market. The number of Contemporary price guides now surpasses the number of Vintage price guides available.

Changing Values

Generally, values for collectible Barbie® dolls go up once they are purchased. However, some do not appreciate and may actually lose

1961 Barbie®
and Ken® dolls
in wedding
attire

#3 Barbie®
doll in Solo in
the Spotlight

value. This is commonly the case for regular-issue Barbie® dolls—dolls that Mattel sells to the general market through most major retail outlets. For example, every year Mattel issues a group of swimsuit-attired dolls for children. While these dolls may be collected, they are not usually viewed as "collectible" and normally do not increase in value.

How values will change for Barbie® dolls over the next few years is uncertain. Vintage dolls commonly appreciate in value about 10 to 15 percent per year, but this figure of course depends on the particular doll. At worst, values for Vintage dolls will likely stay the same. How desirable a doll is during any given year will dictate its actual value. Buying Vintage dolls requires knowledge of the subject, so it can be a risky proposition for uninformed collectors. Vintage-era Barbie® dolls were originally intended for—and generally purchased for—play purposes. Unlike Contemporary Barbie® dolls, relatively few Vintage dolls and accessories were stored away in their original packaging or in pristine condition, so very few in this condition find their way into the secondary market.

Contemporary Barbie® dolls, although easier to find and purchase, can also be risky. Mattel's production of new dolls is enormous. Vintage dolls were released as toys for children, not collectibles, so few examples remain in immaculate condition. However, it is common for Contemporary dolls to be kept in their boxes, so a great number of the Contemporary dolls being produced are kept in their original, as-issued condition. Available supply, as well as future demand, will affect the value of Contemporary Barbie® dolls in coming years—it all depends on what future collectors will be looking for.

A word of common-sense advice: Do not invest your children's college fund in Contemporary Barbie® dolls! Newly issued dolls frequently stagnate in online auctions, sometimes without getting even a single opening bid. And if you sell your collection through secondary-market dealers, you may get only 30 to 50 percent of the retail value. Dealers need to cover their costs and realize a profit within the retail-price ceiling that the market will accept at a particular time.

On rare occasions, a Contemporary doll's value can skyrocket.

The best example of this is the 1988 Happy Holidays Barbie® doll. It retailed for $30. Twelve years later, it was valued between $950 and $1,000. Most Contemporary Barbie® dolls appreciate in value slowly and steadily. It remains to be seen whether there will be enough future buyers to absorb the dolls that are currently made and held in such enormous quantities. Your best bet is to buy a doll because you want it. If it increases in value, enjoy the bonus!

Examples of Fluctuating Values

The following comparisons are not intended to be a guide to current market prices. Rather, they are provided to illustrate how the values of particular dolls have changed over time.

Common collectibles:

- The Hollywood Legends Collection Scarlett O'Hara dolls (four in the series). Each doll originally retailed for $70. At the time of this writing, each doll is valued from $30 to $97.
- The 1996 Gap doll originally retailed for $45. It is now valued from $45 to $75.
- The 1991 Holiday Barbie® doll originally retailed for $35. It is now valued from $120 to $248.

Rare collectibles:

- The 1959 #1 Ponytail Barbie® doll, brunette, originally retailed for $3. It is now valued from $5,848 to $8,300.
- The 1964 Swirl Ponytail Barbie® doll originally retailed for $3. It is now valued from $1,000 to $1,500.
- The 1966 American Girl Barbie® doll originally retailed for $3. It Is now valued from $2,800 to $3,500.

The ease of collecting through the Internet has impacted prices in recent years more than any other factor. Before the Internet, collectors had to search shows and auctions for Barbie® dolls, and prices were based on localized supply and demand. Collectors in various parts of the country may not have had access to shows, so they were often willing to pay more to get what they wanted. With the Internet, collectors all over the world now have an opportunity to bid on the same items at the same time—and the overall effect has been to bring prices down.

Areas of Saturation

During the late 1980s and throughout the 1990s, Mattel focused its product development on new dolls for the adult collector. The good news for collectors is that Mattel began producing higher-quality products and gathering input from Barbie® doll collectors. The bad news for collectors, however, is that the market has become saturated with these collectible dolls, many of which have depreciated in value due to high-volume production. In response to this situation, Mattel announced new production guidelines in 1999. Collectors can now make their purchases knowing that worldwide production of Limited Edition dolls will be kept to 35,000 or fewer, while Collector's Edition dolls will number 35,000 and up.

While most high-volume Contemporary dolls reflect soft resale prices, the 1997 Harley-Davidson Barbie® doll is a notable exception. Initially, these dolls were available only through Harley-Davidson dealers and Toys R Us. Almost immediately, this doll

1994 Barbie® as Scarlett O'Hara from *Gone with the Wind*™

COLLECTOR'S COMPASS

Whether you're buying Vintage or Contemporary Barbie® dolls, exercise caution. When buying Vintage dolls, be aware that sometimes restoration work may have been done that is not always noted—or even known—by the seller. And restoration work always affects the value of a doll.

In other cases, dolls may be incorrectly identified. Sellers of Contemporary Barbie® dolls sometimes exaggerate a particular doll's potential value by comparing it to the relatively few Contemporary dolls that have increased dramatically in value. Collectors who fall for these ploys almost never earn their money back through reselling.

As you become an avid Barbie® doll collector, you may find bargains that you just can't pass up. Often these will be items that aren't perfect but will serve as "placeholders" until you find examples in better condition. If you're convinced that the price is great, figure that you can likely get your money back at a later date. But remember: in the case of Vintage items, prices have remained stable for the past several years. If you pay too much, you may have to wait a long time to get your money back.

became desirable outside the core collector market. It's possible that many motorcycle enthusiasts' collections feature a lone Barbie® doll sporting Harley-Davidson colors—a prime example of collectible crossover interests at work. Prices of these dolls have hit their peak, but have yet to come down significantly. The current value of the 1988 Happy Holidays Barbie® doll is about $800, while the 1997 Harley-Davidson Barbie® doll remains steady at about $500.

As with any collectible, you should buy what you like and enjoy most. If the doll you buy turns out to be an excellent investment, all the better. Just remember that value appreciation is pretty much a roll of the dice—just because one doll in a series increases in value, it doesn't mean they all will.

Easy Come, Easy Go

One collector started buying the Happy Holidays Series in 1988 simply because she thought the doll was pretty. She continued to purchase the latest Happy Holidays Barbie® doll every year. When the price of her 1988 doll skyrocketed to $1,000 in 1995, she cashed in her entire Happy Holidays Barbie® doll collection. Although the other dolls did not command the astonishing resale value of the first doll in the series—in fact, many had not increased in value at all because of high production—she managed to make a great profit. Of course, it doesn't always work out that way. The same collector also bought the Hollywood Legends Collection—also because she liked how they looked—but she ended up selling them two years later for less than she paid for them.

1994 Happy Holidays Barbie® doll

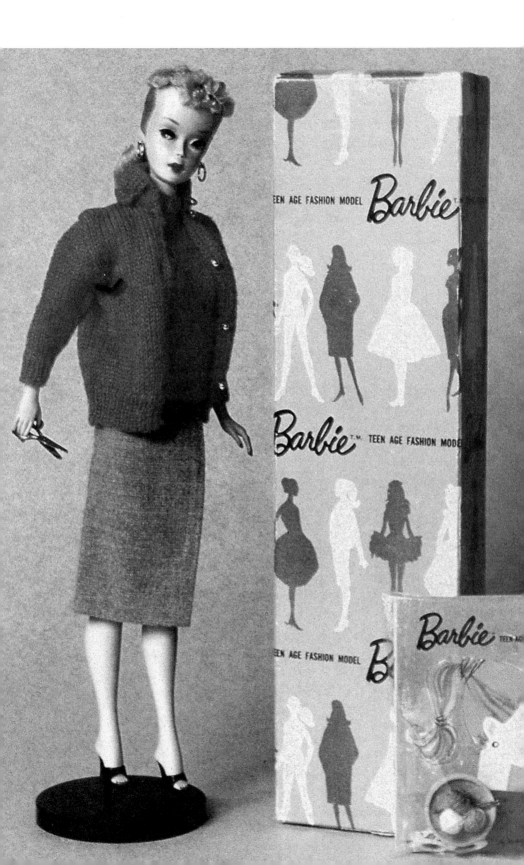

THE HISTORY OF BARBIE® DOLLS

Beginnings

How did the doll that became cherished by a generation—and generations that followed—get its start? The initial inspiration was a young mother's desire to create a three-dimensional version of her daughter's beloved paper dolls. That desire took form when the mother encountered a doll modeled on a saucy German comic-strip character of the 1950s. In that moment, the legendary Barbie® doll was conceived.

Matt-El

In the mid-1950s, Ruth Handler was no ordinary mother, but the co-founder of Mattel, now one of the world's leading toy manu-facturers. In 1945, she and her husband Elliott Handler had formed their company, which was originally conceived as a gift-ware business, with a friend, Harold Matson. They named the company Mattel: "Matt" for Matson and "El" for Elliott. When Matson became ill in 1946, the Handlers bought him out and kept the Mattel name.

Several years went by before any toys were made. The first toys Mattel produced were doll furniture Elliott designed for a 10-inch

opposite:
Ponytail Barbie®
doll in Sweater
Girl, with
Silhouette Box

doll, such as Little Miss Revlon, which was a typical size of that time. These pieces were fairly well received, and they can still be found at toy and doll shows and auctions.

The Inspiration

As young parents, Ruth and Elliot were prime candidates to run a toy company. The industry-proclaimed "whiz kids" derived much of their inspiration from observing their own two children. Ruth, who headed up marketing for Mattel, watched her daughter, Barbara, play for hours with paper dolls—dressing the two-dimensional beauties in their high-fashion dresses and accessories and acting out scenes with them. By contrast, Barbara showed little interest in her baby dolls, which were the prevalent type of doll marketed to little girls in the 1950s. Ruth surmised that Barbara was typical of many little girls her age in that she preferred the glamorous, grown-up fantasy world of her paper dolls over rehearsing for motherhood with her baby dolls.

Armed with this insight, Ruth began to think about a new kind of fashion doll. Miss Revlon, a popular doll of that period, had gone part of the way. While the Revlon doll had an extensive wardrobe, its face and body retained a childish appearance. Ruth wanted the complete fashion look. Her doll would have beautiful clothes made of luxurious fabrics, but would not have the childish body type of the Revlon doll. A trip to Switzerland in 1956 finally brought the idea to conception.

There, Ruth encountered an 11-inch adult female doll dressed in a smartly detailed costume—and the doll was selling very well. Lilli, as the doll was named, was based on a popular cartoon character whose adventures appeared in the German *Bild* newspaper. The cartoon character had been created for an adult audience, but Ruth re-created the concept for an American market and transformed her into an all-American teenage girl. Thus, the Barbie® doll, named for Ruth's daughter, was born.

The Dream

Ruth had lots of ideas about how the Barbie® doll and her wardrobe should look. She wanted the doll to be beautiful, with gorgeous clothes and accessories. She envisioned breathtaking designs for wedding gowns and evening gowns in sumptuous fabrics, complete with tiny snaps and buttons. Tiny purses, shoes, and jewelry would add to the fantasy. The way Ruth saw it, mothers could buy their daughters one doll, then purchase additional outfits. Ruth had the foresight to know that some of her doll's outfits would not fit everyone's budget, so she also planned a less-expensive line of cotton outfits that would come with as many accessories as their chic counterparts.

Ruth was a marketing genius to be sure, but a designer of fashion dolls she was not. So who would ultimately make Ruth's fashion ideas a reality? Elliot contacted the Chouinard School of Art in

Swirl Ponytail in Fashion Editor

Pasadena, seeking a talented designer who could make doll clothes. As a result, Charlotte Johnson was brought on board. At first, the male executives at Mattel were skeptical that the doll would pan out. So Charlotte began her career working part-time during the evenings on her tiny fashions. But as the concept of the Barbie® doll took shape, Mattel hired Charlotte fulltime. She remained an employee of the company for many years. Charlotte was obsessed with detail, and her eye for style and quality produced miniature works of art that captivated children then as they do adult collectors now.

The Barbie® doll and her fabulous wardrobe were initially manufactured in Japan. Ruth traveled to Japan to start the manufacturing process, but it was Charlotte who actually lived there, teaching workers how to root hair, paint faces, and make clothes. It took almost three years of preparation for Ruth's idea to be introduced to the world.

A Trendsetter

By the time Ruth set her ideas in motion, Mattel, Inc., had already become the third-largest toy company in the country. Mattel was producing many toys, but most targeted boys' interests. The time was ripe for the Barbie® doll, as girls also demanded toys carrying the Mattel brand. This was the era of the telephone-book-sized Sears & Roebuck and Montgomery Ward Christmas catalogs, among others, which presented hundreds of toys from which to choose. Barbie® doll would be a fresh alternative to the traditional doll offerings. No one would have ever seen anything quite like it before.

In the minds of marketers at Mattel, the Barbie® doll would open up new vistas for the toy world, though the opportunity was not apparent to retail buyers at first. The Barbie® doll made its debut in March 1959 at the annual Toy Fair trade show in New York City. The buyers were mostly men, and Barbie® doll was not well received. Some big accounts, Sears & Roebuck among them, declined to carry the doll because she seemed too provocative for little girls. However, those who made the leap of faith and ordered the doll were richly rewarded. By summer, the first edition Barbie® doll and her initial selection of twenty-two outfits were flying off the shelves. This success was in large part due to the marketing savvy and determination of Ruth Handler, a pioneer in mass marketing toys to children and their parents.

Did You Know?

More than 105 million yards of fabric have been used in Barbie® fashions, making Mattel one of the largest apparel manufacturers in the world.

Thanks to Ruth, Mattel was one of the first toy companies to advertise on TV. They started running ads for their other toys in 1955 on the *Mickey Mouse Club* show and by the late 1950s were advertising on all three networks. With this approach, Ruth brought the Barbie® doll directly to her consumers. In addition, Mattel commissioned a marketing study, which found that children responded positively to an advertising message that presented Barbie® as a real person rather than a mere doll. The appeal of fashion role-playing that Ruth originally observed with daughter Barbara and her glamorous paper dolls had been confirmed.

Because of the TV ads, the Barbie® doll became the first "must have" toy. Little girls everywhere loved the fashionable doll, and moms, like it or not, were eventually persuaded to buy them. Even mothers who were initially put off by the Barbie® doll's adult look were won over by Mattel's presentation of the doll as a way to teach their daughters proper dress and grooming. They hoped Barbie® doll could be used to turn little tomboys into little princesses.

The first Barbie® doll was 11½ inches tall with a white-tone body and rooted silky hair. She had a ponytail, curly bangs, and came as either a blonde or a brunette. She wore a black-and-white zebra-print swimsuit, gold hoop earrings, sunglasses, black mule shoes, and was perched on a round pedestal with two prongs to stand her up. The original Barbie® dolls were packaged in a white, two-piece cardboard box, which was imprinted with some of the outfits that could be purchased separately for the doll. Barbie® doll fashion catalogs were inserted in

1959 #1 Barbie® doll in Resort Set with pink silhouette box.

Pretty in Pink

Some early Barbie® dolls were dressed in one of the twenty-two outfits then available and were packaged in pink silhouette boxes produced exclusively for retailers. These fully outfitted dolls were meant for display in the stores and were never intended for sale to the public. Barbie® dolls in this exclusive packaging are rare and are coveted by Vintage collectors today.

Two #1
Barbie® dolls

the packages as an additional enticement to buy outfits. She retailed for a whopping $3.00!

The First Barbie® Dolls

Today, the first version of the doll shown at the 1959 New York Toy Fair is known as the #1 Barbie® doll. Because relatively few were ordered, few were manufactured, thus making this the most desirable and highest-valued doll in today's Barbie® doll collecting field.

In 1960, changes were made to the Barbie® doll, and the pedestal stand, which had proven problematic, was changed to a wire stand that held the doll beneath the arms. The face and hair remained the same. This is known as the #2 Barbie® doll. Later in 1960, a #3 Barbie® doll was released. Her eyebrows were softened from the inverted V shape to a more delicate arch, and her eyes were given blue irises, though her hair remained the same. In 1961, a new hairstyle marked the "Bubble Cut" Barbie® doll.

Since that New York Toy Fair in 1959, Mattel has introduced many new editions of Barbie® dolls. The Barbie® doll's popularity almost immediately produced offshoots: her boyfriend, a doll named Ken®, named after the Handlers' son, was launched in 1961, and her girlfriend, a doll named Midge, came on the scene in 1963. A little sister, Skipper doll, came out in 1964. Today, Barbie® doll has an even larger range of friends and family.

TM

COLLECTOR'S COMPASS

Although Barbie® doll is the most popular doll to collect, many collections have been built around the Skipper doll, the Kelly® doll (another little sister), and the Ken® doll! There are drawbacks to collecting a relatively minor niche, however. While such items may be abundant and cheap, if you ever decide to sell them, you may have difficulty finding many interested parties willing to pay top dollar. The number-one rule of collecting is to buy what you like, but remember, you might own that item for a long time if others don't find the same appeal in it that you do.

Durability

Barbie® doll is a durable toy. The early dolls have withstood the passage of more than forty years without much deterioration. Usually, time takes its toll on the doll's hair and clothes, but if the body is properly cared for, it can remain in like-new condition.

Barbie® Doll Bodies

Barbie® doll bodies have been manufactured using several different types of vinyl and vinyl-molding methods. The original Barbie® doll was made by a method of molding vinyl known as rotocasting. Many molding techniques were tried to get the first Barbie® doll correct. It was important that the body size and shape remain exactly the same year after year so that clothes would fit properly. Plaster molds failed because of shrinkage. Finally, a zinc alloy mold proved successful. Charlotte Johnson was a perfectionist, and although hand shape and finger placement were not important to the clothing fit, these details were also given close attention.

The Barbie® doll's hair, made of Saran fiber, was originally hand rooted, and the bodies were assembled in Japan. More contemporary versions have hair stitched on by machine. The doll's face is spray-painted on through a mask template.

Common Casualties: Barbie® Doll Hair, Clothing, and Accessories

It's difficult to find older Ponytail Barbie® dolls with hair in pristine condition. Children were usually tempted to take the ponytail down to brush the doll's hair—only to find that the scalps were rooted only around the outside hairline. The center of the head was completely bald! They'd try to retie the ponytail, but rarely did a child achieve the same "factory" perfection.

The first Barbie® doll clothing, made from fur trim, richly lined brocade, satin, and simple cotton—with real buttons and zippers—was hand finished by Japanese housewives. All the accessories, including tiny metal scissors that opened and closed, small wooden bowls with balls of yarn and knitting needles, pearl stud earrings, drop necklace and matching pearl snake bracelet, were perfectly executed in miniature. These tiny items were prone to

Midge doll, Allan doll, Ken® doll, Barbie® doll

loss during play, and it's rare indeed to find any early Barbie® doll complete with every accessory that was originally included in the package.

Although doll collectors today can and should enjoy displaying Vintage Barbie® dolls, be aware that the outfits are fragile. They may fade or discolor if exposed to light and dust, and extensive handling will also soil the clothing. Never be tempted to wash Barbie® doll clothing; laundering reduces value more than soil in most enthusiasts' eyes.

Another condition that affects the early Barbie® dolls over time is called "green ear." The earrings the doll originally wore were made of brass, which often tarnished and stained her vinyl earlobes green. If these earrings are left on the doll over a long period of time, the discoloration can spread to large areas of the doll's face and neck. While measures can be taken to remove some of the green, even a trace of this condition greatly reduces the value of many a Vintage doll. There are many more factors that affect the value of a Barbie® doll. We'll look at them more closely in "Determining Barbie® Doll Value."

Did You Know?

Among the pieces encased in a time capsule during the 1976 Bicentennial celebration were several Barbie® dolls.

From Concept to Collectible

Barbie® doll collecting started over twenty-five years ago, and although collectors have come and gone, there are a few enduring reasons why people collect the dolls: some collect for investment, others collect for display, while others collect the dolls to bring back childhood memories or to bond with other collectors.

As a group, the first Barbie® doll collectors are Baby Boomers— Barbie® doll was their childhood doll. And whether they collect the Vintage or Contemporary Barbie® dolls, these collectors are buying back their childhoods. They may regret that they let their parents sell their dolls at yard sales or give them away. Or, if they still have their childhood dolls, they may have only parts of the original outfits because they traded clothes and accessories as a

---

Bringing the World Together, One Doll at a Time

Barbie® doll collecting has connected people across the world. Take the case of a collector-turned-dealer who started selling more than ten years ago. Early on, she had made contact with a doll dealer in Japan, to whom she sold lots of dolls and outfits. But over the years, she lost touch with him. Recently, she placed several Barbie® doll items up for auction on the Internet. When a winner in the auction e-mailed her to complete the transaction, he asked if she was the same person from whom he had purchased Barbie® items all those years ago. Turned out, he was the same dealer in Japan!

> ### *The Barbie® Hall of Fame*
> Although most Barbie® collections are in private hands, there was a privately operated Barbie® Hall of Fame museum in Palo Alto, California, in which more than 20,000 dolls were displayed—along with structures, cars, and related Barbie® doll items. In early 1999, Mattel purchased this collection from its owner, Evelyn Burkhalter, with the intention of preserving it in a corporate museum currently being planned.

child. Thus, they collect to bring the dolls back to their original state of completeness.

The first detailed Barbie® doll encyclopedia was put out in 1977, but by that time, the collecting boom was well on its way. Collectors in significant numbers began appearing in the mid-1970s. Many collections were begun as an activity between mothers and their daughters. By the 1970s, many little girls who had grown up with Barbie® had children of their own. What better way could a mother connect with her child than to introduce her to the doll she'd played with and treasured in her own childhood?

1960 Barbie® Austin-Healy Sportscar manufactured by Irwin

TM

STARTING YOUR COLLECTION

Ways to Begin

If you're interested in starting a collection, you can go in a number of directions. Your local bookstore's "Antiques and Collectibles" or "Hobbies" section will likely have at least a few books—perhaps several—on Barbie® dolls, both Vintage and Contemporary. You might want to browse through our list on page 38, or the more comprehensive listings in "Recommended Books" (page 138), to help you sort through them. If your bookstore has a magazine rack, look for Barbie® doll–enthusiast magazines. Many newsstands and magazine departments in supermarkets also carry these publications.

Check your local library's database card catalog. If you don't find what you're seeking on the shelves, ask your librarian to do an interlibrary search for you. You'll be amazed at how much information a resourceful librarian can turn up for you in a few days.

If you're an Internet user, you've got a world of Barbie® doll collecting right under your fingertips. Do a keyword search on "barbie" using your preferred search engine, and you'll soon be scrolling through pages of "hits" on the name. Some of these will take you to the many auction sites on the Net. If you do a keyword search at any one of these auction sites, you'll find a wide array of

opposite:
Bubble Cut
Barbie® doll in
Solo in the
Spotlight, with
rare Suzy
Goose piano

35

Barbie® doll material for sale. You can also click on "completed auctions" to see the winning bids on auctions that have already closed. Your induction and education into the world of Barbie® doll collecting has already begun!

Once you've begun to search and research, you'll likely quickly develop an appetite to tap into the physical world of Barbie® collecting. Like most other collectibles, this doll has an exclusive community. But by presenting yourself to the world of Barbie® doll collecting as someone who appreciates the doll and has taken time to inform yourself, you're bound to gain entrance to circles of similarly dedicated Barbie® doll fans. Keep in mind, most major collections reside in private hands. Many advanced collectors remain fairly tight-lipped about what they own. However, there are many avenues to explore to begin amassing a collection of your own.

You'll be well served to start with an all–Barbie® doll show that gives you exposure to many dolls at once. Have you decided yet whether your collecting tastes lean to Vintage Barbie® dolls or the Contemporary editions? There's nothing like seeing scores of both "in the flesh" to help you focus your interests.

The first Barbie® doll convention was held in 1980, but since then a Barbie® doll show has been hosted every year by a local Barbie® doll club. The conventions feature seminars, fashion shows, salesrooms, and showrooms, giving collectors a chance to talk about their favorite doll with each other and to meet representatives from Mattel. Convention packages sometimes feature

COLLECTOR'S COMPASS

Never buy until you feel ready to make a purchase. Do your homework, both before and after you make the purchase. Don't rely on dealers to direct your collection; they may—intentionally or not—steer you toward what they have to sell. Only when you've built up relationships with reputable dealers will they begin to watch for your interests and help you build the collection you desire. And always, always, buy the very best you can afford.

#3 Ponytail
Barbie® doll
with Allan
doll dressed
in Wedding
Day Set

special dolls offered by the club or Mattel, as well as other goodies, which are available only to attendees.

General doll shows are usually not as productive when you're just starting out, because you're not likely to find a wide variety of Barbie® dolls in that setting. There may be only one dealer who has both Vintage and Contemporary dolls at large general doll and collectibles shows, and perhaps several with an assortment of Contemporary dolls.

Another way to tap in to the community is to join a Barbie® doll club. There are many such clubs throughout the United States and the world where collectors meet to trade, learn about, and play with Barbie® dolls. Clubs vary in size, organization, and policies, such as whether a newsletter is printed or whether they accept new or out-of-state members.

Move slowly before joining any club. Go to a few meetings and quietly observe what goes on. You'll be able to get a sense of the club's dynamics before you make a commitment to join. When all is said and done, you might find that the club scene is not for you and that the Internet, books, and magazines satisfy your information needs.

The Best Resources for Collectors

There are numerous reference materials for Barbie® doll collectors—novices and advanced collectors alike. The following explain some great places to start. "Resources" (pages 133–137) features all kinds of resource information, from dealer listings to Web sites and everything in between.

Magazines

There are a few magazines published specifically on Barbie® doll, but perhaps the best one is *Barbie® Bazaar,* which can be found at most newsstands. In business for more than ten years, this magazine features articles on various topics and covers all aspects of collecting, from newer to older items. One of the best things about *Barbie® Bazaar* is that it usually features a "do-it-yourself" article. A classifieds section and plenty of ads are also included. *Miller's Fashion Doll* is a very popular and extremely helpful magazine that also features value information.

Books

Two large Barbie® doll collections sold by Theriault's auction house were documented in catalogs that have become reference books in and of themselves: *Theriault's Presents Barbie®* (Florence Theriault, Gold Horse Publishing, 1985) and *Barbie® Rarities* (Florence Theriault with Sarah Sink Eames, Gold Horse Publishing, 1992). Look for copies of these catalogs for sale at Barbie® doll shows.

Luckily for Barbie® doll collectors, there are lots of references available for tracking down styles and fashions as well as for learning the history of the doll. Price guides including A. Glenn Mandeville's *Doll Fashion Anthology and Price Guide* also provide a lot of history and background on style and fashion. But for filling in the gaps and doing your detective work, also have a look at Kitturah Westenhouser's book, *The Story of Barbie®*, which is a complete history of the Barbie® doll, her family, and outfits from 1959 through 1989. This volume also includes a handy, complete section on cleaning and revitalizing your dolls and their clothes. If earlier Barbie® doll clothes are your passion, seek out *Barbie® Fashion, Volume I*, by Sarah Sink Eames, which is a complete history of the wardrobes of Barbie®, her friends, and her family from 1959 to 1967.

The *Collectors Encyclopedia of Barbie® Dolls and Collectibles* by Sibyl DeWein and Joan Ashabraner was one of the first guides to the Barbie® doll and friends from 1959 through 1976. Collectors have declared this volume indispensable, as it chronicles the markings for each doll manufactured between 1959 and 1976.

Everything you ever wanted to know about Barbie® dolls is contained in *The Ultimate Barbie® Doll Book* by Marcie Melillo, which collectors everywhere have touted as a must-have reference. Other great resources include *The Barbie® Doll Boom* by J. Michael Augustyniak, which looks at dolls made between 1986 and 1995 and is essential for collectors of Contemporary dolls, and Sarah Sink Eames' *Barbie® Doll Fashion, Volume II*, a great reference for fashions from 1968 to 1974. Also be sure to check out *Barbie® Doll and Her Mod, Mod, Mod, Mod World of Fashion 1967–1972*, with text by Joe Blitman and color photographs by Kevin Mulligan.

American Girl in Fraternity Dance

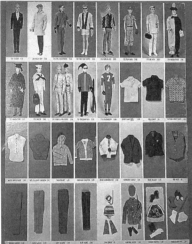

Rare cardboard store
display for Ken® doll
(front and back)

Videos

Oh You Beautiful Doll, produced by collectors Joe Blitman and Kevin Mulligan, is an essential visual reference for new Barbie® doll collectors. This one-hour, full-color video is full of facts and tips for holding your own in the collectors' market, and it also gives great advice for cleaning your dolls, replacing arms and legs, and more.

Web Sites

The Internet has had an enormous impact on Barbie® doll collecting—and mainly for the better. Prices have come down, and the Internet provides an ongoing supply of older items to collectors. Through online auctions and Barbie® doll sites, collectors can find tiny accessories to finish an outfit or find newer collectible dolls.

Mattel has a Web site—www.barbie.com— that is helpful to collectors of newer dolls. Some other sites that include the keyword "barbie" may not be sites about the doll itself, so proceed with caution. In the back of this book, you'll find a list of recommended dedicated Barbie™ doll Web sites you can visit.

The eBay auction site has dozens of classifications for buying and selling Barbie® dolls online. If you want to buy or sell a Barbie® through an online auction, you must first be a registered member—it's free—and then you can post your stuff and bid on others' Barbie® doll auction items to your heart's content. Each piece that you put up, however, will be subject to a small seller's commission, payable to the auction site via the credit card number that you must supply in the course of registering to sell.

The Golden Rules of Collecting Barbie® Dolls

There are guidelines you should keep in mind as you embark on collecting Barbie® dolls. We like to refer to these ten rules as the golden rules of Barbie® doll collecting.

Rule Number 1: Collect What You Like

There is no more important rule in collecting Barbie® dolls than this one. It's hard to go wrong when you buy something you like, because whether it appreciates in value or not, you still enjoy having it around. There is no other way to collect Contemporary dolls, because it's unlikely that you can buy every new edition that Mattel produces. Even if money is no object, you'd quickly run out of space to store and display them.

Rule Number 2: Quality, Not Quantity

It's not how many dolls and accessories you have. It's how many good, treasured, valuable, adored items you have in your collection. Don't buy something just because it relates to Barbie® doll or because it's too affordable to resist. That brings us back to rule number one: concentrate on what you like, not what you think you should buy. Also, if you have no room to display and enjoy new stuff, think twice about buying it. It isn't much fun to have dolls packed away in a closet rather than attractively displayed where you can enjoy them.

Buying every doll in a series is not a wise move, either in a monetary or emotional sense. And it isn't particularly necessary. If you don't like a doll but you buy it anyway to complete a series, you're probably buying it for the wrong reason. It won't make you happy, and if you can't sell it down the line for a substantial profit, it will annoy you as long as you have it.

Rule Number 3: Stay within Your Budget

More than one collector has been forced to file for bankruptcy after a Barbie® doll–buying binge. And to make matters worse, many times the courts have seized all the dolls in the course of proceedings. What good is buying Barbie® dolls if you can't hold on to them? Put your collecting into a price range you can afford.

COLLECTOR'S COMPASS

One way to control your spending is to leave your checkbook, ATM card, and/or credit cards at home. Bring only as much cash as your budget allows. That way, you won't be tempted to spend more money than you intended to.

If you like the older items but cannot afford them, buy Mattel's Vintage Reproductions.

Establish a spending cap for your collection. Make purchasing Barbie® doll items part of your monthly household budget. You don't have to spend all the money you put aside each month, but you should never spend more than this amount. Save part of your allotted amount in anticipation of a big show or convention. And if you've got your eye on a pricey Barbie® doll item, go a few months without spending anything. "Bank" this savings toward your expensive purchase. The discipline you learn may very well add to your enjoyment of the doll once you own it.

Rule Number 4: Keep Your Head

When it comes to Barbie® doll and fashion shopping, put a price limit on each item you want to buy. Remember, unless you are buying the extremely rare items, there will almost always be another if you pass up the one that you know is overpriced. It's easy to get carried away when you're in competition for an item you've had your eye on for a while. But don't get ahead of yourself! Whether you're bidding at an auction, responding to an ad, or scanning the tables at a Barbie® show, keep that maximum price figure emblazoned on your brain. The more experience you get with these events and with seeing what items go for, the more realistic you'll become about limiting your spending for Barbie® dolls. Don't let self-inflicted buying panic turn your joy in collecting into regret later on.

Rule Number 5: Knowledge is Power

Learn all you can about what you are collecting. This is where many collectors fail. Often, they think that talking with dealers will expose them to all they need to know. While dealers enjoy talking about Barbie® dolls, and some may be extremely knowledgeable, they often don't have time to explain all the ins and outs of Barbie® doll collecting. Also, unless they are specialized, experienced dealers, they just might not know everything. It's up to you to do the careful reading and research that will give you a solid grounding in the field.

You might be reluctant to spend money on reference books when you could spend it on dolls. While that's understandable, it is a mistake not to invest in a good reference library. How else will you be able to recognize that a doll lying on a table at a flea market with a $5 tag is actually worth $300? Without the proper knowledge, you're bound to fall victim to more than one bad purchase—and you may pass up a great one.

Remember that books aren't the only or the definitive source of information. Price guides are just that: guides. Give yourself some firsthand experience before you buy. If you are collecting Vintage items, go to doll shows and look at the range of outfits and dolls. Handle them (with the dealer's permission, of course), note their strong points and flaws in their condition, and compare what different dealers are asking for them. There is no better teacher than direct experience. And you can look, ask questions, and learn all you can at a show for the price of admission.

Rule Number 6: Be Cautious

In a face-to face transaction with an unfamiliar dealer, you should have your questions answered, gain assurances that your satisfaction is guaranteed if you buy, and have a positive "gut feeling" that the person with whom you are dealing is reputable. If you are buying by some remote method—from an ad, by telephone, or over the Internet—you need to double your caution. All of the above applies, as well as making sure you don't put money at risk before you know what you're getting. If a deal seems too good to be true, it probably is. Here are some suggestions:

- Request a clear photo and description of every item you're contemplating buying.
- Pay by credit card, if possible. Credit-card companies will intervene on your behalf if you decide to dispute the transaction.

Ponytail Barbie® Music Box Ge-Tar

- Have the items shipped Collect on Delivery (C.O.D.). This option guarantees that you receive the goods before paying.
- Arrange some other payment plan with the seller (partial payment, partial shipment; third-party escrow agent; etc.)

Rule Number 7: Honor Your Commitments

You must stand by your word when you make a commitment to a dealer. Because doll dealers have had so many problems with collectors ordering a new-edition doll, then reneging when they spot it in another retail store, many demand nonrefundable deposits before accepting an order. The dealer has to defray various costs to get a product for you. She deserves integrity from you as the buyer for providing that service.

If you make a commitment, stick with it—both for the sake of your own reputation and the sake of your relationship with a dealer who may be able to help you when a doll truly is hard to find. It pays to be ethical. The Barbie® doll world is a small one, and word gets out quickly when someone isn't honorable or reliable.

COLLECTOR'S COMPASS

Don't beat yourself up if you make a bad decision early on—or even after years of collecting. No matter how long you collect or how knowledgeable you become, mistakes are inevitable. This is just a fact of collecting. Learn from the mistake so you don't repeat it.

Rule Number 8: Be a Friendly Competitor

Make collecting "friends." Few things are more enjoyable to Barbie® doll collectors than talking about Barbie® dolls. Friendships made in the Barbie® doll collecting world can last a lifetime. But sometimes competition makes collectors tense and reserved. Try not to get caught up in this mean-spiritedness. Pass along information and help when you can. If you assist others, they will likely look out for you.

Additionally, you should establish a network. Let friends and neighbors know about your interest in Barbie® doll collecting. You may be surprised by the number of people who call you with dolls for sale. Train yourself to ask people the right questions in the right way to find out exactly what they have.

Rule Number 9: Be Patient

Good things come to those who wait. It may sound clichéd, but in the Barbie® doll world, it's a rule to live by. If you have to be the first one on your block to own the latest Barbie® doll, you'll pay for the privilege. Sometimes if you wait just a few weeks, you can get a bargain. Also, feelings of competitive urgency may cloud your judgment in making wise buying decisions. Don't fall for the hype of an advertised shortage or "rarity." Be smart; move slowly. The money you save will add up. Once you know the true rarities among Barbie® dolls, you can relax, knowing that you're likely to see the more common ones again and again.

1961
#5 Ponytail

#3 Brunette

#5 Ponytail

45

Rule Number 10: Keep Good Records

Always ask for a receipt for your purchases. It's important for insurance purposes and for tracking expenditures, and essential if you ever resell. You should also keep a written inventory. This will pay off if you decide to sell, upgrade, or put a rider on your insurance policy. A small, spiral-bound notebook may be all you need. If you have a computer, you can use it to build a database. Pertinent information should include

- Date you purchased an item
- Where and from whom you purchased it
- Stock number, completeness, and condition of the item
- The price you paid for it

The Marketplace

The marketplace for Barbie® doll is vast, and there are many venues for purchasing Barbie® dolls. The ones you'll choose to explore first will depend on what you're looking for. The ones you continue to use will be determined by what you find, what you're successful in buying, and what holds your interests. For example, if you're thinking about collecting older items, your best bet is to seek out other collectors who may be looking to upgrade or sell off duplicates. When a collector begins to specialize in one area, she is more apt to want to sell her now-undesired items to free up space and money to pursue her specialty.

Whether you're buying Vintage or Contemporary Barbie® dolls, where you decide to buy your dolls will depend on several factors, including how much money you are willing to spend. The secondary market is the only way to find Vintage dolls, but think twice before buying Contemporary dolls through this venue. Almost any toy store, department store, or discount store is a great starting place for a new collector interested in Contemporary Barbie® dolls. Special-edition dolls may be manufactured for just one retail chain, like J.C. Penney, Target, or Toys 'R' Us. Some dolls are available only through Mattel, while others are doll-shop exclusives.

Vintage dolls can be found through doll shows, auctions, secondary-market dealers (including mail order and online), and on the odd occasion, at garage sales. Unlike the almost unlimited

COLLECTOR'S COMPASS

Following is a list of abbreviations and terms to guide you on your way to correctly identifying Barbie® dolls and their accessories.

- NRFB (never removed from box)
- MIB (mint in box)
- MIP (mint in package)
- M/C (mint and complete)
- M (mint)
- NM (near mint)
- Exc. (excellent)
- G (good)
- P (poor)
- PM (primary market)
- SM (secondary market)
- DM (direct mail)
- SASE (self-addressed stamped envelope)
- DSLSASE (double-stamped large self-addressed envelope)
- LE (limited edition)
- SP (special edition)
- DSS (department store special)
- HTF (hard to find)
- SL (straight leg)
- BL, b/l (bent leg)
- CT (closed-toe shoe)
- OT (open-toe shoe)
- Hard curl (a hard roll of hair found at the end of a ponytail)
- Mute (a talking doll that does not talk)
- No bend (the knee joint is sprung)
- Neck split (the head's neck hole is torn)
- Paint rubs (missing areas of facial paint)
- Ponytail wrap (hair is wrapped around the top rubber band of a Ponytail Barbie®)
- Tnt (Twist 'N Turn™ Barbie® doll)

quantities available of most Contemporary dolls, the number of Vintage dolls in collectible condition is limited. Therefore, competition may be fierce and prices high for the choice pieces.

Garage, Tag, and Yard Sales

Newer Barbie® dolls are often found at these sales, but it's rare to find Vintage dolls here. If you are lucky enough to find one, you can be fairly sure that the seller doesn't know what she has. Sometimes if you ask about older items, the seller might bring out older Barbie® dolls that she didn't intend to sell—but may. You never know. Overall, trying to find Vintage dolls this way is a waste of time when there are better avenues to explore. Whether you're seeking Vintage or Contemporary dolls, have a price guide handy to verify values before you buy.

Estate Sales and Estate Auctions

Estate sales and auctions are better places to find Vintage dolls. The sellers often advertise the contents of the sale or provide a phone number for inquiries about whether specific items will be featured. Prices are usually in line with the market, and the company running the sale is probably familiar with values in the Barbie® doll collecting world. Show up early and get a number if they are being handed out. When Barbie® dolls are included in a sale, they tend to go quickly, so you should try to be one of the first inside. Professional dealers and their "pickers" frequent estate sales and auctions. The action will be brisk for prime pieces most of the time.

Auctions are always a surprise. Given the right people bidding, prices can soar to incredible heights. At the same time, less desirable items can go for a fraction of what they may fetch in another setting for lack of interest among the attendees.

Flea Markets and Bazaars

If you've done your homework, you can sometimes find good bargains at flea markets. They can be good sources for newer dolls, although the sellers are generally a mixed bag. Some are knowledgeable about the merchandise they're offering and the prices they're asking, and some are not. Barbie® doll items frequently show up at these locations, but they may be mislabeled; newer

continued on page 65

Ponytail Barbie® doll
in Friday Night Date

Barbie®

DOLL

PHOTO GALLERY

1970 Barbie® doll
in Rainbow Wraps

1968 Hair Fair
in Snug Fuzz

Francie d
in Concer
the Park

Barbie® doll in
her first
sports car, an
Austin-Healey

1961 #5 Ponytail

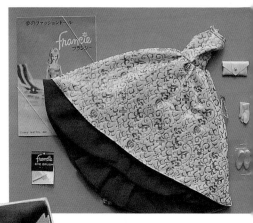

Francie gift set made for the Japanese market

Francie doll
made for
the Japanese
market

1997 Chinese
Empress Barbie
doll from the
Great Eras
Collection

**1995 Bob Mackie
Goddess of the Sun
Barbie® doll**

**1997 Billions
of Dreams
Barbie® doll**

55

**#2 Barbie® doll
in Picnic Set**

Left to right: Ponytail Barbie® dolls in Easter Parade,
Gay Parisienne, and Roman Holiday

1968 Twist 'N'
Turn doll in
Travel in Style

1997 Barbie
Millicent Roberts
in Perfectly Suited
business outfit

ir Happenings in maxi and midi

1980 Black Barbie® doll, the first African American Barbie® doll

1970 Talking Barbie® doll in Magnificent Midi

99 40th Anniversary Barbie® ll. The black and silver dice echoes the original rbie® doll's striped bathing it. Included with the doll is miniature replica of the 1959 ckaged doll.

Vintage Mix 'n Match Set box

1961 Ponytail in Golden Elegance

#2 Barbie® doll in Commuter Set

American Girl in It's Cold Outside

1993 Bob Mackie Masquerade Ball Barbie® doll

1989 Happy Holidays Barbie® doll

A 6-foot Barbie® mannequin welcomes Busy Gal auctiongoers in Washington, D.C.

continued from page 48

dolls may be priced much higher than they should be. There are very bad deals to be made by the unwary and unknowledgeable. It is still possible, however, to discover a Vintage Barbie® doll that might actually be worth $150 marked $25 at a flea market.

Thrift and Secondhand Shops

For the most part, thrift and secondhand shop owners have a fairly good sense of what's valuable and what isn't. This doesn't mean they don't occasionally overlook a "gem." However, these venues are generally about as hit-and-miss as garage sales. You can waste a lot of time searching and end up with nothing.

Consignment Shops

Rather than buy the items outright, consignment shops take in merchandise from individuals and charge a percentage of the selling price as a fee for merchandising the item—usually about 10 to 15 percent or more. The shop may convey offers to the owners of the merchandise, who may or may not sell their items at a reduced price. Often a consignment shop will have a set policy about how long it will display the item before reducing the price by a set percentage.

Although there's a chance you'll find great additions to your collection at consignment shops, don't count on the dealer or seller to know what he has or to price it correctly. Also, never make an unreasonable lowball offer that may be taken as insulting. It's worth cultivating relationships with consignment shop owners, who generally handle a fairly high turnover of new items. The owner may be willing to take your name and contact you when other similar items come in.

Retail and Toy Stores

The most popular place to find Contemporary Barbie® doll items is your local toy store. Twenty years ago, Barbie® dolls typically occupied ten feet of space; today, Barbie® doll items may take up sixty or more feet of space! Working through this venue, collectors can pre-order new releases, take their time in making decisions, and even put their favorite items on layaway. Also, many department stores carry their own exclusive editions of Barbie® dolls not sold elsewhere.

Visit the toy store regularly, look at the range of dolls on the market, and pay attention to what's selling. The shop staff are often quite eager to tell you what's "hot."

You might also try hitting offbeat places like drugstores, which may have old dolls in stock. In some cases, you may be able to find dolls on clearance, marked well below secondary-market prices.

The Internet

The Internet has impacted Barbie® doll prices more in the last few years than any other phenomenon in the last decade. Before the Internet, collectors searched shows and local auctions for Barbie®

The Collector's Toolbox

When you head out for the hunt, arm yourself with the proper tools. Here's a checklist of what you should bring along with you:

- A magnifying glass. Even if you have perfect vision, you might miss tiny flaws that are not easily visible to the naked eye.
- A flashlight. Seeing a potential purchase as clearly as you can is essential. The lighting at most doll shows generally runs from bad to poor, so even a pocket flashlight will be an asset.
- Copies of your "want list." This is good practice for two reasons. For one, it will help you stay focused on the specific items you're seeking. Second, you can leave your want lists with dealers, who may call you if they come across one of your items. Give only your name, phone number, and e-mail address.
- Packing material. Small zippered plastic bags are handy for securing small accessory items that may get lost. Sheets of bubble wrap or a roll of paper towels provide easy temporary protection for your purchases until you get them home.
- A shopping bag with handles. A tote bag or backpack will serve the same purpose.
- A pen and notepad. Take notes and collect business cards. A doll show is a great place to learn about Barbie® dolls. Also, you might see a few items you may want to add to your collection down the road. Having a pen handy allows you to jot down which dealer is carrying what piece. You might also get the phone numbers of some fellow collectors.
- Small bills. If your negotiations with a dealer get down to a one to five dollar increment, it behooves you to come up with the exact change to make the purchase.
- Comfortable shoes—and if you're at an outdoor show, sunscreen and perhaps a sun hat. You're going to be doing a lot of walking.

dolls. Prices were based on local supply and demand. Because collectors in certain parts of the country did not have easy access to these events, they were willing to pay more to get what they wanted. With the Internet, everyone with a computer and Internet access has the opportunity to view everything that's for sale anywhere at the same time. The supply on the Internet is much larger than

---

Preparing for a Show

Megashows, like Brimfield's in Massachusetts or Renninger's in Pennsylvania, require outfitting akin to preparing for an expedition. In addition to your tool kit, take bottled water, a roll of toilet paper and hand wipes (or waterless hand cleaner), snacks, plus any other "necessities" you may require. If you're covering the show with a partner, walkie-talkies may help you stay in touch with each other (though be aware that other buyers with similar equipment may "listen in" to conversations on your channel).

Plan to get up before the chickens to be in line for the choice deals. Some of these huge, multifield shows may offer dealer setup and open shopping at the same time. Or they may have an "early buyers" admission, which might run ten to fifteen times the regular admission price. This premium ticket price goes right into the promoter's pocket and irks many dealers who have to be ready for customers that much earlier. But finding that one great piece may make the inflated admission worth it. Do your homework beforehand and keep focused on your specific wants list. These shows are fast moving, and you won't have time to check your reference books once you're on the field.

---

that available at any single show. The audience is also bigger than that attending any show. The net result of this widening of the market on both sides of the transaction is that prices have generally come down.

Many Barbie® doll dealers have their own Web sites. To find them, type the keyword "barbie" into a search engine. Another great way to find dealers' Web sites is to pick up a Barbie® doll magazine and check the dealers' listings. In addition to addresses and phone numbers, doll dealers generally put their Web addresses in their ads if they have a site. Keep in mind that dealers with Web sites featuring fixed-price lists are there primarily to sell, not to educate. However, you can learn a lot by reading descriptions, studying prices, and looking at pictures of the items for sale. Find *Miller's Fashion Doll* magazine online at www.millersfashiondoll.com and *Barbie® Bazaar* at www.barbiebazaar.com. Both feature great stuff, including current price guides, identification guides, chat rooms, and classifieds. *Miller's Fashion Doll Online* also features an events section, listing upcoming Barbie® doll shows with dates, directions, hours, and dealer-contact information.

Items for sale may also be listed with online collector groups, such as those offered by America On Line (AOL) to its subscribers. Again, be cautious. People sometimes post incorrect information. Educate yourself before deciding to purchase through this venue. As is the case with any auction, prices are subject to the enthusiasm of the bidders. We'll look closely at Internet auctions later in this section.

Ads in Trade Papers

Ads are a good way to find odd items, but proceed with caution. Ask the seller to provide a picture of the item and a detailed history, as well as references, before you commit to buy. Check the magazines for information on rarity, condition, and factors that affect the value of a doll. Never just send money to anyone whose ad you answer. If the seller is nearby, pay her a visit in person if you're considering making a sizable purchase.

TV Shopping Channels

These are often good sources for discounted dolls, although some-times the information provided is inaccurate. Because of the large quantities of a product required to satisfy demand on a TV shop-ping channel, most of the dolls sold there will not likely increase much in value. Be cautious of claims made by the hosts, who are often ignorant of the market, and ignore the admonitions of "call ins," who urge viewers at home to buy before it's too late.

Clubs, Societies, and Associations

Collectors' clubs are a preferred place to buy dolls. These organi-zations often sponsor local Barbie® doll shows that can be great places to buy items from reasonably knowledgeable collectors who generally ask fair prices. Clubs can be good places to sell and trade with other collectors, but there may be political rivalries. If you prefer the anonymity of cyberspace, there's an internet club that boasts over two hundred members.

Dealers

With the amount of Barbie® doll items on the market today, your safest bet is to buy from reputable dealers who stand behind their merchandise. Good dealers note any restoration work they're aware of on Vintage dolls, and they describe the flaws in both dolls and outfits in detail. Again, the collecting community is really an intimate society, and word gets out quickly about dealers who scam customers. That doesn't mean that dishonest people don't show up from time to time. It's a good idea to start out with modest purchases until you are comfortable with a dealer's integrity. If a reputable dealer senses that your hesitance may come from distrust, she may offer you some references of satisfied customers.

Don't mistake the dealer for your friend, however. She's running a business and speaks to many collectors each day. Keep your conversations brief and polite, and concentrate on getting answers to your questions. Gush over your collection with other collectors.

If a dealer specializes in Barbie® dolls, chances are he knows what he's selling. It's legitimate to ask a dealer how long he's been in business, what shows he does, or if he's a collector himself. If a dealer is a collector, he might have more insight about the field than someone who's exclusively a dealer.

Dealers who simply dabble in dolls may not have done the research necessary to price a doll correctly. In many cases, their dolls are overpriced and mislabeled. For example, an uneducated dealer may think that all Ponytail Barbie® dolls are #1s, and price them accordingly. It's not that she's deliberately trying to mislead you; it might just be that she doesn't know the difference herself. On the other hand, an educated dealer might also underprice dolls or clothes. As with any collecting field, it is up to you to study, to know what you are looking at, and to have a good idea of its correct value. If you don't trust a dealer, don't buy from him or her.

Collect business cards and make notes about what different dealers carry. As you get to know other collectors, ask them about the dealers they use and why. Most collectors will be glad to point you in the right direction.

Ask a dealer what he knows about where a doll may have come from and if any restoration work has been done. Before values skyrocketed, people generally left their dolls in as-is condition. As the supply of dolls in excellent condition dried up, more and more dolls were restored. Hair was re-rooted and faces were touched up or repainted. Even if it doesn't matter to you, you should know if a doll's been restored so you can relate that information to your buyer if you ever decide to sell it. In some cases, a dealer might not know a doll's complete history because it has passed through many hands. Be sure to ask the dealer to let you examine the doll if you have doubts.

Ask the dealer her terms of purchase before you commit to buy. Generally, most new dolls in original packaging are not returnable. However, most dealers will accept returns on new dolls if there is a legitimate problem, for example, if an item was left out of the box by Mattel or if it was damaged during shipping (if you're buying by mail order or online). Most dealers will accept Vintage items returned in the condition they were sent within a specified number of days—usually five—of receipt. Honest mistakes can happen. It's a good idea to start from this premise when dealing with a problem, at least until you find out otherwise.

Be cautious about whom you believe when determining whether an item is complete or not. Similarly, one dealer may describe an item as mint while another will describe the same piece as near-mint. The difference may be a matter of one or the other's

COLLECTOR'S COMPASS

Do not ask dealers to knock off the sales tax. This is a fast way to anger a dealer and quash the potential for a future relationship. As in any business, doll dealers may be audited for possible sales-tax infractions. If a dealer chooses not to charge you sales tax, it's her legal obligation to net out any tax applicable from the amount you paid. Whether she does or not is between her and the department of revenue of the state in which she's doing business.

If you've obtained a resale certificate from your state, it's appropriate to ask the dealer to exclude the sales tax from your purchase. In that case, the dealer should record your tax number on the receipt.

sensitivity to what constitutes "perfect" condition. There are errors in some of the best reference books. And seemingly helpful collectors may offer advice or opinions as a matter of fact that turn out to be way off base.

The Dealer's Market

You can work with dealers to find the items you're looking for in a number of ways. Keep in mind that having a relationship with one or more specialized dealers is almost a necessity for Vintage collecting. Once you've found a good dealer and established a relationship, stay in touch regularly—whether in person or by other means. Chances are, she will start to look for items for you. If you're a Contemporary collector, you may meet one of many doll dealers who buy new releases direct from Mattel and offer these lines to their best customers on preferential terms.

Mail or Phone

Get satisfactory answers to all the questions you have, including the seller's terms of sale, before making a deal by phone. Whether you buy by phone or through the mail, you will be asked to send a check first. And the check will have to clear before an item is shipped. If you send a money order, the dealer will probably send the item right away. Include a written statement about any understandings you've agreed to with the seller—return privilege, condition as stated, accessories included, et cetera—with your payment.

Legs of 1968
Twist 'N Turn
Barbie® doll

If you are not happy with the item upon receipt, call the dealer immediately to explain the problem and ask to return the item. If you discover later that the item is damaged or is not authentic, it's your problem. Keep in mind that if you are buying Vintage, you are not likely to be buying a flawless doll. Older dolls have usually been played with, so buy only what you are willing to live with. But by all means, expect the seller to live up to his end of the bargain in every way.

You will be responsible for the shipping in both directions. If you do not return the item in the same condition as it was received, you may not get a refund. For example, if you have a Ponytail doll and you take the ponytail down, do not expect a refund. Never take NRFB dolls or outfits out of the box and expect to return them. Few new dolls will be returnable, unless you've established a clear understanding with the seller at the time of purchase.

When there's a level of trust between dealer and collector, buying on approval is sometimes allowed. This practice of having a doll sent to you to preview before you buy is usually done only with Vintage items. You and the dealer should have agreed upon a price at the time the doll is sent; it's generally not good practice to negotiate after you've received it. If you decide to buy, you send the dealer payment. Otherwise, you return the doll in exactly the same condition, securely packed and insured, within the agreed-upon time limit.

Independent Shops

Look in the yellow pages under "dolls" to locate shop dealers in your area. Frequently, storefront dealers will negotiate prices, but be respectful and don't expect the kinds of discounts typical at shows and flea markets. There's significant overhead to running a shop, and owners simply don't have the same kind of pricing "wiggle room" as transient dealers.

The main advantages to buying through shop dealers is that you'll be able to actually see an item before paying for it, something not possible when buying through the mail. Also, shop dealers will likely stay in one place for at least the duration of their lease, making them a more stable source of potential supply for your collecting.

Antiques and Collectibles Malls

Antiques and collectibles malls may be located in former grocery stores, factories, warehouses, or even barns. The selling area is divided into aisles with numerous booths or locked show-cases. The display spaces are rented to various dealers and are serviced by roving mall staff, who may be employees or dealers. These staff members will unlock a case to show you an item upon request. They're not likely to be knowledgeable about the inventory in the mall, unless it happens to be their own merchandise.

You pay at a central checkout, where an employee collects all sales receipts and taxes. The mall operator remits the proceeds of sales to the respective dealers, retaining a commission to cover the overhead of merchandising and servicing their sales.

Buying through an antiques or collectibles mall permits you to examine items for sale in a much less hectic atmosphere than that of a show or flea market. They're often productive venues for hunting, as you can view many dealers' offerings in one place.

Also, mall operators often require dealers leasing spaces to change out their unsold stock periodically in order to keep the merchandise fresh. That makes repeated trips to the malls in your area worthwhile.

Discounts are usually restricted to a nominal amount. Taking 10 percent off the tagged price is common. If you wish to make a lesser offer, the mall staff will usually relay it to the individual dealer, who may or may not accept your price.

Antiques and Collectibles Shows

Doll shows are held in cities across the country several times a year. The problem with these shows, however, is that unless the dealer specializes in Barbie® dolls, items are frequently mislabeled and mispriced. Just because someone has set up a booth at a show doesn't mean they know what they are doing.

Arrive early and plan to pay an admission fee of $2 to $10 for the day. Focus on what you came for. Be a comparison shopper. Start by taking a quick tour of the whole floor and see what the dealers are offering. Make mental or written notes of any items of interest to you. Then go back and narrow down your attention to the prime candidates on your want list. You may find that there are several examples of a doll you're seeking being offered by different dealers. Take the time to compare condition, completeness, and asking prices before negotiating for a single item. When you comparison-shop, you do run the risk of your first choice being snapped up by someone else, but keep in mind that if you don't make the best purchase today, there'll always be another show— and another chance to buy the doll you want.

If you arrive early, you can chat with other collectors while you wait to be admitted. You may get lucky and run across a person (usually not a collector) who's brought her own dolls to the

show to sell to dealers. If approached nicely, this person may sell the dolls to you. And when the show starts, you'll be one of the first inside.

Barbie® dolls for sale

Fire codes limit the number of people permitted in a commercial space at one time, and if you arrive after opening, a crowded show may keep you waiting outside until enough people leave for you to be admitted. In that time, the best items may be sold.

Dealer Fixed-Price Auction Catalogs

Dealers and auctioneers advertise in Barbie® doll publications and in doll magazines. You often get on their mailing lists by subscribing to a magazine or ordering an auction catalog from one of their ads. Many catalog and fixed-price dealers charge for subscriptions, but it's common for them to send you one or more sample catalogs as an inducement to purchase from them as well as to subscribe to the catalog. Because printing and mailing are expen-

sive, many of these catalogs are migrating to the Internet, where color images and detailed descriptions can be attractively presented at much lower costs.

Use the same precautions and actively ask questions about the merchandise when you begin buying from catalog dealers, just as you should with any seller who's new to you. Reputable catalog and fixed-price dealers publish their terms of sale right in their catalogs and sales sheets.

Pricing and Negotiation Guidelines

Dealers don't pull prices out of the air. They know what they paid for an item, what work and additional expense was necessary to prepare it for sale, and the price they must obtain to turn a profit. But they may buy items and price them with very specific objectives in mind:

- Sometimes a dealer purchases an item at a premium price because it is highly desirable. Presenting it adds luster to the rest of her inventory as a "traffic builder." She'll likely put a prestige price on it, as well.

- Sometimes an item comes along in a group lot, and the dealer simply wants to turn it over quickly to get her cost back plus a small profit. She'll price it accordingly.

- A dealer may deliberately mark up a highly desirable item exorbitantly, hoping that some collector desperate to have it will come along.

- An item may have been sitting in a dealer's inventory for too long, and the dealer will price it to move so she can refresh her stock. Often dealers sell and trade among themselves to achieve this end.

Negotiation on price is a highly individual matter with dealers. Some simply are not open to negotiation, while others may indicate their willingness to bend on price early in your conversation with them. Some may reduce the price only if a large multiple-item sale is involved.

Whatever the circumstances, your politeness is essential. Do not tell a dealer a price is too high. Asking "Are your prices negotiable?" is a much less confrontational approach. If she says no, you can either buy anyway or walk away. The choice is yours.

Under no circumstances is it appropriate to criticize the merchandise as a negotiating ploy. If you don't like what's being offered at the price being asked, say thanks and walk away. You've preserved the potential to do business with that dealer on another occasion. Rudeness will only leave the dealer with a bad taste that she may well remember at your next encounter.

One of the reasons that dealers may be reluctant to negotiate is that they've got a lot of "opportunity cost" in the items they're selling. This is often the case with Vintage items. For instance, a dealer may have to pay three or four visits to someone with a collection to sell before sealing a deal. Sometimes, a dealer angling for a collection has it sold out from under him to another dealer, and all the time and work involved are lost. Or maybe the supplier changed her mind and decided to keep her collection in the end. Or worse, maybe she really just wanted a free "appraisal" and never had any real intention of selling. And then there are the issues of theft and bad checks at doll shows.

Most dealers willing to negotiate will be able to take only about 10 percent off their price because of overhead. If the price you have in mind is close to the dealer's price, politely ask: "I had X dollars in mind to spend. Would you consider my offer?" Do not insult the dealer with an offer of 50 percent of the price. If a dealer is going out of business, he might be able to do better than 10 percent off the price marked.

The general rule is that prices of items in a fixed-price catalog or sales list are not negotiable. It is acceptable to politely ask at a show, but expect a refusal if the show has just opened or the item is highly desirable. The best time to negotiate prices at a show is near closing time when dealers are faced with packing up what hasn't sold. If it hasn't been a particularly successful show, they may be mentally calculating how much more they need to sell just to cover their costs. Proffering your low bid in these circumstances may seem like taking advantage of someone's loss, but the beauty of free enterprise is that the choice to do business, or not, is always in the individual's hands.

Auctions

Depending on your appetite for pressure and competition, auctions can be an exciting way to obtain the pieces you want for your collection. Here we'll give you the ins and outs, and the dos and don'ts, for buying Barbie® doll items at auction.

Online Auctions

Online auctions have revolutionized the collecting world in the past few years. All you need is a computer or Web TV connection to the Internet, and you're on your way.

The mother of all online auction sites, eBay, has thousands of listings for Barbie® doll, but eBay isn't the only site. To find other auction sites, type "barbie auction" into any search engine. Most auction Web sites have a separate Barbie® doll category. You can also search for specifics by typing in "harley davidson barbie" or "Bob Mackie barbie," for example.

American Girl in Fashion Luncheon

It doesn't cost anything but time to browse, but if you want to bid, you have to register with the site by providing your name, street address, and e-mail address. After you supply the necessary information, you select a screen name, which can be different from your e-mail address if you like. You will also need to select a password. After you register successfully, you'll receive an e-mail giving you a green light to start bidding.

Before you bid on any item, check out the seller's feedback. What is feedback? When a transaction occurs, the buyer will post a feedback note briefly describing her dealings with the seller for the benefit of other would-be bidders. The seller might also post feedback about the buyer's promptness in paying, communication, and soon.

Online Auctions: Pros and Cons

Pros:

- You can bid from the comfort—and anonymity—of your own home.
- Most sellers provide color photos of the items, which are often better than information available in online and printed catalogs and sales lists.
- The feedback mechanism provides public notice of unreliable dealers (and buyers),
- Rare, difficult-to-find items sometimes show up.
- Online auctions are perfect for small dealers or individuals with just a few things to sell, because the auction provides them with access to a larger group of buyers than they could otherwise reach.

Cons:

- You can't see the item in person.
- Not knowing the parties you're buying from can be a bit nerve-wracking.
- Sellers lacking knowledge may not describe an item accurately.
- You need to observe the auction's user agreement and rules of conduct judiciously to avoid negative feedback or even exclusion from the auction. This shouldn't be a problem for you, but even benign negligence is not tolerated; you must fulfill your commitments reliably in order to remain in good standing.

Having negative feedback as either a buyer or seller is deadly in the online auction world. If you garner a certain number of negative comments, many of the auctions will exclude you from participating for a period of time as punishment for being unscrupulous or unreliable.

The most common way to bid online is to wait until the last several hours before the closing time to place your bid. Some people even wait until the last seconds, which is called "sniping." Snipers hope to place the highest bid before someone else can top them to win the auction.

Their efforts are frequently foiled by "proxy bidding," however. If you will be unavailable to bid when the auction ends, you might consider this route. Simply put, proxy bidding means that you enter the maximum amount you are willing to bid for the item. The auction computer then bids on your behalf, increasing your bids by the auction's prescribed increments as other bidders top it, up to your maximum. Thus, a sniping attempt may fail because the computer bidding as your proxy will automatically top a sniped bid if your maximum hasn't been reached. The system will never bid your maximum until it is absolutely necessary. In other words, if your high proxy bid is $25, and the last bid is $18, the computer will not offer $25, but the next increment after $18.

In some cases, a seller may put a reserve price on an item. This means that he has set a minimum he'll sell the item for. The

Rare factory updo in Debutante Ball

reserve price is typically hidden from bidders until it's reached in the bidding. The screen will then read "reserve met" after the current high bid. If the seller does not obtain his reserve, he does not have to sell the item.

If you are the winning bidder, you and the seller will be notified by e-mail. You and the seller will then be responsible for arranging the completion of the transaction, which includes payment arrangements, shipping, and what have you—all done by e-mails.

Live Auctions

Most people find live auctions exciting. Some find them exasperating. Others don't like them at all. A well-publicized auction presenting a strong offering—perhaps the contents of an important collection—can draw bidders from far and wide. The competitive atmosphere can be highly charged. A top auctioneer knows how to whip up the energy level even further with lively banter and by hammering down the lots at lightning speed.

If you've never attended an auction, by all means go to one and take in the flavor of the event. But as a beginner, you'll be well advised to sit on your hands this first time out. Live auctions are probably the most likely place for even a seasoned collector to overbid for an item because competitive juices can flow so strongly.

The significant Barbie® doll auctions are usually listed in Barbie® doll or general doll magazines. Local auctions are listed only occasionally in the national magazines. For them, you need to check your local newspapers as well as antiques and collectibles malls and doll shops, which usually post flyers of upcoming auctions and shows. The phone book has listings for local auction houses, which frequently will

TM

COLLECTOR'S COMPASS

It's best not to be the opening bidder. If the auctioneer can't raise a bid at his starting price, he will keep dropping the price until someone bids. Watch what happens with a few items before you start bidding.

> ### *Live Auctions: Pros and Cons*
> **Pros:**
> - Items can be viewed before purchase, and once paid for, immediately taken home.
> - Rare items often appear in these auctions.
> - An advanced collector may sell his collection in this manner, because it is a fast and efficient way to dispose of many items at once in a competitive setting. It's not unusual for auctions to carry the name of a recognized collector's holdings as part of the draw, for example, "featuring the 25-year collection of so-and-so."
>
> **Cons:**
> - It is easy to get caught up in the heat of the moment and pay more than you should for an item.
> - It is easy to miss flaws and problems during the preview period.

add your name to their mailing lists and/or make note of your particular interests.

A major auction by one of the major houses will usually feature a catalog for sale, published well in advance of the auction. Use it to preview the lots to be auctioned, research values, and decide what you want to bid on. The catalog will list the auction rules and types of payment accepted. If you plan to pay by check, a letter of credit from your bank will probably be required. Know the rules before you attend an auction. Auctioned items are offered "as is, where is." They are not returnable, and you are responsible for getting them home, so make plans in advance for any shipping.

Decide your maximum bids before you even go to the auction. Stick to your decisions. When setting your bid ceilings, remember that auction houses often charge buyers' premiums (up to 20 percent) on top of the winning bid. You'll find them explained in the auction catalog. Be sure to take the premium into account in your maximum bid. Also, don't forget the sales tax.

Most auctions have a preview period, giving bidders time to examine the items up close. Many auctioneers will not allow you to handle the items, however, so you will have to ask auction staff for assistance. Examine the items carefully, make notes, and adjust your bids, if appropriate, based on what you've found. Sometimes auctions allow "room hopping" at a hotel designated for out-of-town bidders. This means that dealers attending the auction will bring items to sell from their rooms. Signs at the hotel will direct you to where to find these rooms (often booked on the same floor). Room hopping is a kind of "side show" to the main event. It can be fun, but be careful not to let such shopping eat up your budget for the auction bidding that you've carefully prepared for.

Registration takes place at the entrance of the auction hall. You will provide your name and address and other personal information, as well as your method of payment. You will be given a paddle with a number to use for bidding. The universally acceptable way to place a bid is to raise your paddle. The auctioneer will call your number and urge other bidders to increase over your bid. The bidding is usually closed by the phrases "Fair warning. Going once, going twice, sold!"

A cataloged auction normally follows the catalog order, which allows you to take breaks between lots on which you plan to bid. But the speed of an auction is fast and can be unpredictable; don't stray too far away from the action.

You are free to go whenever you want during the auction. When you are ready to leave, pay the cashier and pick up your winnings. Some auctioneers will take Visa and MasterCard, but charge a fee. The preferred method of payment is with cash.

Absentee Bidding

Cataloged live auctions almost always offer absentee bidding. If you want to place absentee bids, fill in the absentee bid sheet with your top bid for each item. You may also be required to furnish a Visa or Master Card number, or even to send a deposit in advance to guarantee you are a serious bidder.

Absentee bids are generally executed as if you were at the auction. Someone from the auctioneer's staff will be assigned to bid for you, or the auctioneer will execute your bids by proxy from the podium. If the bidding stops before your maximum is reached, you win. Note that the auctioneer will bid your maximum only

#3 Barbie® doll in Sweet Dreams

when another bidder takes the bid to the level at which your maximum would be the next bid increment.

Sometimes you can bid personally by telephone. You need to indicate this as your preference when you submit your absentee-bid form. One of the auction staff will call you as your desired lots approach and stay on the line with you during the bidding, advising you of the current high bid and executing your bids as you instruct him. If you win, the same rules apply as for live bidders and bidders who've placed winning absentee bids.

Mail and Phone Auctions

Mail and phone auctions are usually listed in Barbie® doll and general doll magazines and some toy publications. Like absentee bidding, you must first purchase a catalog, at which time you'll be assigned a bidder number. Read the descriptions and carefully examine the photos. Call the auction house with any questions. Be sure to read the rules completely, as every auction is different. As in absentee bidding, you have to fill out a bid sheet, which lists your initial bid for the items you're interested in. The catalog also features the exact time the auction closes. Each auction has individual rules about how long the auction may continue past the official closing time. After the close, winning bidders will be invoiced by mail, and your winnings will be shipped upon receipt of payment. The total you're billed will be the amount of your bid, a buyer's premium (if stated in the auction rules), shipping and insurance, and state sales tax if the auction takes place in the state in which you reside. As in a live auction, items won through a mail or phone auction are not returnable, unless explicitly stated in the auction rules.

Most mail bidding starts low unless a bidder will not be able to call in on the closing day to check or raise her bid. The real action of the auction occurs on closing day, and in the final hours, bidders may phone in every few minutes to make sure they're still holding the high bids. It gives you a huge advantage to have a telephone with an automatic redial button if you get caught up in this frenzy. You'll be getting a lot of busy signals as bidders vie for

open phone lines. Some auctioneers provide a call-back service to advise you if your bid has been surpassed; they may or may not charge to do this (check the auction rules).

Keep in mind the auction bidding tenets that we've stressed throughout: Do your homework and get answers to your questions before the auction closing day. Read and understand the rules of the auction beforehand. Set your maximum for each lot that interests you and stick to it (include the buyer's premium if applicable). We'll say that again: set your maximum and stick to it.

Vintage Ponytail Barbie® dolls in their original packaging. Courtesy of Rosalie Whyel Museum of Doll Art. Photo by Charles Backus

85

DETERMINING BARBIE® DOLL VALUE

Factors That Determine Value

Many factors go into determining the value of a Barbie® doll. In this section, you'll learn how to tell a potentially valuable piece from one with little to no value.

Condition

Most Vintage Barbie® dolls were originally bought for a child's enjoyment. These original owners weren't concerned with the future value of their toys. Clothes were sometimes roughly taken on and off, hair came down to be restyled, or dolls may have been treated to a haircut. Because of such factors, condition plays a major role in determining the value of Vintage Barbie® dolls. A doll is most collectible when it's a highly desired edition in the best possible condition.

With Contemporary dolls, condition will most likely be good or better. Many of these dolls were purchased to be collected. The condition of the box might significantly affect value if it is creased, dented, or crushed. The doll inside and her clothing and accessories may have been harmed if a hole in the box has allowed air or dirt to enter and damage the clothing. Such a doll that may have

opposite:
1967 Barbie® doll
in Shimmering
Magic

TM

COLLECTOR'S COMPASS

Formalized grading of condition is fairly new to the Barbie® doll collecting world. Check the list on page 47 to see common abbreviations for the condition of Barbie® dolls and accessories. Here's an example of how condition plays a role in Contemporary Barbie® doll collecting: If a doll or outfit is NRFB (never removed from box) but the original cellophane has been cut or is missing, the value will be reduced from the NRFB price by 10 to 15 percent. If the outfit or doll is in mint condition, but there's no box, reduce the NRFB price by 45 to 50 percent. If the outfit or doll is in excellent condition with all pieces intact, reduce the NRFB price by 60 to 75 percent. If the outfit or doll is in only good condition, reduce the rate by 90 to 95 percent. So, for example, if a doll is worth $1,000 NRFB, a doll with no box in mint condition would be worth $550. The same doll in excellent condition would be worth $250, and if it's only in good condition, it will be worth from $50 to $100. In poor condition, the same doll might only be worth $10 to $25.00. Condition is also sometimes based on a 10 to 1 rating system that is commonly applied to antique toys:

- C-10: Mint, just as it came from the factory
- C-9: Near mint
- C-8: Excellent
- C-7: Near excellent
- C-6, C-5: Good
- C-4: Average
- C-3, C-2: Poor
- C-1: Junk

been considered "Mint in Box" might end up being graded in "Very Good" or even just "Good" condition.

Vintage dolls are a little trickier to grade. Most commonly, a doll or outfit is found in good—not mint or excellent—condition. Even if it was a former play toy, it might have the majority of face paint and all its hair, fingers, and most of the original outfit intact. Chances are, however, that it will not look "factory fresh." If it does, you may have reason to suspect that it has been restored, whether or not it is identified as such. Restoration can affect the value of a doll—and not for the better, as we'll explain.

It is common to find Vintage dolls shy an original accessory or two—or even missing a whole outfit. For example, you may find a dress without matching shoes or jewelry, or a collectible-condition doll offered for sale without any clothes. Tiny pieces of jewelry and shoes may have fallen victim to the vacuum cleaner, or various accessories may have been separated from their original dolls as children received new outfits to dress them in. Therefore, dolls that remain complete with original outfits and accessories are more valuable and rare. Vintage dolls that were not taken out of the box are about ten to fifteen times more valuable.

Condition will be a variable consideration, depending on why you are collecting Barbie® dolls. If you are collecting with the hope that your dolls will appreciate in value, research and collect only the most rare items in the best condition you can find. If you are collecting to recapture your past, a doll that shows signs of the love and attention it received from its original owner may endear it to you.

Damage

Depending upon its nature and extent, damage can greatly or minimally affect the value of a Barbie® doll. The storage of dolls and outfits was not considered important until recently. Lucky Contemporary Barbie® dolls that have been kept out of direct sunlight and away from other extremes of heat and humidity are usually only minimally damaged. But Vintage dolls' clothes may have faded or been damaged by dust, dirt, mildew, and other factors. These dolls may have only recently been rescued from uncaring storage at the bottom of a box in the garage, basement, or attic. And early collectors may not have realized that the outfits of dolls displayed on open shelves could deteriorate over time.

Some damage cannot be helped. For instance, the metal inside a doll's legs may sometimes turn the legs green. Also, many collectors of dolls made in the 1960s (Ponytails and Bubble Cuts) left in the little pearl earrings, and over time, the ears turned green. Some damage, such as fading, is not reversible, but collectors have found ways to make it less noticeable.

This section explains the most common types of damage to Barbie® and how they affect the value of the doll. Keep in mind that individual collectors can judge items differently. One person may be very turned off by a flaw, while another will be willing to overlook it because the doll holds some overriding appeal for her. Whatever your inclination, understanding how damage and flaws impact value will give you an idea of how much to expect to pay for a doll that's in less-than-perfect condition.

Bowed Legs

This condition usually occurs because of improper storage. Sometimes a doll is squashed into a box or storage case that is slightly too short. If it is stored that way for any length of time, the legs may become bowed or bent. If the doll is from the late 1960s to early 1970s, the joints in the legs may be broken so the legs no longer bend. These conditions are, for the most part, irreversible.

Extra Earring Holes

Early Barbie® dolls were packaged with earrings in their ears. When children took the small earrings out, it was not uncommon for them to create new puncture holes by forcing the earrings through the vinyl. This somewhat reduces the value of the doll, but not dramatically.

Greasy Face

Barbie® dolls manufactured in 1961, both Bubble Cuts and Ponytails, have a shiny vinyl skin, which is sticky to the touch. There's no way to fix the problem as it's a defect in the vinyl formulation used to manufacture those dolls. Because they are unattractive, they are less valuable than even many later-model dolls.

Green Ear

Earrings that came with the early dolls were made of brass, which tarnishes. When dolls are stored with the earrings in place, the tarnish will stain the vinyl around the earring green. If the earrings are left in place over a long period, the green may engulf the doll's entire head and neck or even spread to the body. This flaw is a huge issue for nearly everybody and greatly reduces the value of a doll.

Hairstyle Damage

It is difficult to ruin a Bubble Cut's hairstyle because it was meant to be combed. This is not the case with the Ponytail Barbie® dolls, however. Many have lost some value because someone took the ponytail down and couldn't put it back in its original style. It's a bigger problem if the hair has been cut or some is missing. The hair can be pulled out fairly easily if it is combed roughly. Look for empty root holes in the head. If the doll has been given a haircut—however artful—the collectible value is diminished enormously.

Irregular Skin Tone

When not stored properly, the highly desirable Ponytail #1, #2, and #3 Barbie® dolls can turn a ghostly white color, which reduces their value significantly. Also, dolls produced during Mattel's lean years in the 1970s and early 1980s may have white dots on the skin as well as greenish staining on the legs, a result of the metal used inside.

Missing Fingers and Toes

Sometimes fingers will be missing or toes nipped off. This is a less serious defect if the doll is a common body, which can be fairly easily replaced. However, this can greatly affect the value of a rare doll.

Ponytail black vinyl cases

Missing Paint

Wear to the facial paint and nail polish is a very common problem that affects the value relative to how blemished the doll's appearance is. Normal wear and tear can cause paint to rub off eyebrows, lips, eyelash ridge, and finger- and toenails. Even minor paint wear can cause a substantial decrease in the value of a rare doll.

Mold and Mildew

Dolls stored in dark, damp, warm conditions are likely to be damaged by mold and mildew staining and will acquire a musty odor that's hard to remove. Even worse, a single mildewed doll can infect your entire collection if they're stored together. "Quarantine" any new acquisitions that show signs of mold or mildew to avoid an epidemic. Seek the help of a professional doll doctor to treat any ailing dolls you may own. Unchecked and untreated, the condition is usually deadly to a doll's value.

Neck Split

This flaw is usually the result of rough treatment when a doll's head has been removed—whether to replace it with another, to clean it, or to switch bodies. What-ever the cause, split neck is one of the worst fates that can befall a Barbie® doll. If the neck is ruined, the doll is ruined.

Nose Nips

A nip or dent at the end of the nose is sometimes difficult to see head-on, so be sure to inspect a doll in profile to check for this condition. Although it may seem minor, this kind of damage can have a huge effect on the value of the doll.

Split Shoes

Sometimes the shoes of Vintage dolls will split when placed on a doll's foot too roughly or when left on a doll in storage. Once split, the shoes have no value. Mismatched shoes will also affect the value.

TM

COLLECTOR'S COMPASS

Never mix the old with the new. It is always frowned upon in Barbie® doll circles to display reproduced pieces with original Vintage dolls. In fact, because of the potential for confusion among novice collectors, most dealers do not display reproductions anywhere near their Vintage items.

Stains on Feet

Red, black, and navy shoes may stain the doll's feet if left on for an extended period of time. This problem can usually be remedied and only slightly affects the value of the doll.

Torn or Dirty Clothing

Torn clothing is usually an indication of all-around poor condition. Repairs can be made, but the value of the clothing will be greatly diminished. Also, it is better for an original Barbie® doll outfit to be a little dirty than to be washed. When clothes are washed, colors bleed and fabric shrinks, which affects fit. In other words, the doll's value will be washed away with the soil in her clothes. When in doubt, leave it alone.

Missing or Replaced Parts

A doll with its original outfit and all accessories is obviously the most desirable example in all cases. If a dealer is selling a doll without the shoes, and the collector can easily find a pair of the correct ones for a modest price, then the value of the doll is not diminished much by being less than complete. If the doll is missing its head, and an original head will be difficult to find and probably quite costly, the body might not be worth much. Such an item could be priced low and in mint condition, but have no takers, because the educated collectors know the missing piece is unlikely ever to be acquired.

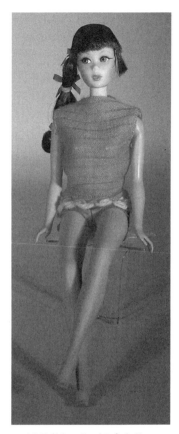

1968 Talking Barbie® doll

Functional Versus Nonfunctional

Luckily, most Barbie® dolls don't do anything mechanical, so function isn't usually an issue. Some dolls were manufactured with special mechanical features, but these are not generally collected. One of the first examples is the 1968 Talking Barbie® doll. The talking mechanism was not well made, and at best worked only briefly. Additionally, the limbs were not firmly attached. Even those dolls not removed from their original packaging usually do not talk, and often the arms and legs are lying at the bottom of the box, with only the head and torso strapped in place. Like other Vintage dolls, the value of this doll has, over time, gone up. But these severe

1971 Talking Barbie®
gift set

structural problems have kept the relative value lower than other Vintage Barbie® dolls.

Basket Cases

Some Barbie® dolls have been loved to death or woefully neglected. They are completely worn or damaged beyond any possible collectible value. However, they can be useful for their parts. Many collectors purchase "basket cases" to make minor repairs to better dolls. For example, if a collector purchases a doll in otherwise excellent condition that has broken fingertips on one hand, she might use a basket-case body from the same year that has perfectly matching nails and vinyl tone to replace the arm on the nearly perfect doll.

Basket cases may also be used—without their heads—as dress forms to display clothing. Or they may be used for experimental purposes, for instance, to test a technique for treating green ear or for restyling a doll's hair. You have nothing to lose with these dolls.

In the last few years, a growing number of collectors have been restyling and designing their own dolls. They take basket cases, strip the makeup, pull the hair out, and start with a bare doll. Then they do their own thing to customize the doll's personality and wardrobe.

Repairs and Restoration

A restored Vintage doll may be offered at a high price because a dealer spent a lot of time and money preparing the doll for market. That doesn't mean the doll is high in value. What's acceptable in terms of repair and restoration depends on the collector. Some may flatly refuse to buy anything restored, while others prefer a well-done repair to a defect. A collector who can't live with a tiny dot of missing lip paint will say restoration is the way to go. For purists, however, dolls should remain untouched. There are many restored dolls in the marketplace. You need to decide for yourself what you find acceptable.

The most common restoration work is re-rooting the hair—one hole or an entire head of hair—or restyling it if a ponytail has been taken down. Face repainting is also popular. In the best examples, the work has been performed with such skill that it is difficult, if not impossible, to tell it's not original. Always ask the seller if the item is restored. A reputable dealer will identify the dolls that have been worked on.

When the Barbie® magazines first appeared, collectors freely contributed tips on how to restore hairstyles, deal with soiled clothes, restore face paint, and clean doll bodies. However, not all of these collectors' recommendations have proven to be sound. A reliable source is "The Care and Repair of Teen Dolls" in *A Fashion Anthology & Price Guide* by A. Glenn Mandeville. Some dealers and collectors have hung out shingles as "doll doctors" specializing in the repair of dolls and their clothes. You'll find them advertised in the Barbie® magazines. If at all possible, get a referral from a fellow collector who's already had a positive experience with one of them before entrusting a valued "patient" to the doctor's care.

It's important to note in your records when you have an item repaired. Take before and after photos. Get and keep the receipt from the doll doctor. If you decide to sell the doll, have the history at hand. It's not fair to other Barbie® doll collectors to keep silent about any repairs or restoration, and a faulty memory is no excuse. You'll also want to include the cost of repair as part of your expense in marketing the doll when you file your tax return for the year in which you sell it.

Original Packaging

Original boxes are highly desirable for Vintage Barbie® doll collectors. Most were discarded, so they are relatively rare. The value of each box varies from doll to doll. Vintage boxes are sometimes sold separately and can range in cost from $35 to $500. The early boxes have wonderful period-fashion illustrations. Look for bright graphics (no fading), no staining, no split box corners, and end flaps in place.

Boxes are not normally reproduced for collector use, although the cardboard liners found inside the boxes often are. These are available through dealers and at shows.

Original price tags and stickers, if present, should be left undisturbed. They neither add to nor reduce the value of the box; however, if they are very large they may obscure some of

Shoes and purses, mint in package

On Parade
gift set

the box graphics and make the box undesirable. Usually they add a touch of irony. Imagine an original $3.00 price tag on an item that may sell for hundreds or thousands of dollars today.

The 1960s dolls featured a foil-paper wrist tag that identified them as genuine Mattel items. This was done in an effort to differentiate the Barbie® doll from the many copycat dolls that appeared after the Mattel doll's initial release. The foil tags were easily removed so most dolls no longer have them. The tag can add from $25 to $200 to the price of the doll, depending upon the rarity of the doll.

Aesthetic Value

Beauty is an important factor in the desirability of a particular Barbie® doll. Face paint screening varies with Vintage dolls. Sometimes a face can look particularly harsh, which can turn off collectors. On the other hand, the more vivid paint colors used during the mid-1960s add to the premium prices these dolls fetch.

Mattel has released Barbie® dolls for almost every imaginable occasion, but the dolls will not be desirable for their commemorative significance alone. Collectors are attracted to the beauty of a well-executed piece—the face, the hair, the magnificent wardrobe. However, even if a doll is spectacular, the value will remain low if it was produced in large quantities.

Personal Value

Personal memories can make a Barbie® doll desirable. Likewise, recollections of the time can be just as significant for individual collectors. For example, the Bubble Cut Barbie® doll released in 1962 had a bouffant hairstyle that emulated Jacqueline Bouvier Kennedy's. Jackie was a tremendously popular First Lady, and a Bubble Cut doll with her signature pillbox hat holds great appeal for people who still adore the era of Camelot. The sophisticated fashions of the early 1960s are reflected in the elegant beaded gowns and rabbit-stole outfits created for Barbie® dolls during that period. Barbie® doll fashions also followed the mod scene from 1967 to 1971. The dolls' long, straight hair, short skirts, and long dangly earrings still attract a large number of fans. If a Barbie® doll collector is nostalgic for a period, chances are she's collecting the dolls that were released during that time.

Age

Barbie® dolls are dated by their markings. With time, you should be able to recognize Vintage heads on sight. Just remember, the date marked on a Barbie® doll is not necessarily the date of manufacture or production; it is the copyright date. *The Ultimate Barbie® Doll Book* by Marcie Melillo is a valuable guide to the several markings typical of dolls manufactured for United States distribution. Original marks are located on the right side of the hip, in raised lettering. For instance:

Barbie®

Pats. Pend.

©MCMLVIII

by

Mattel

Inc.

Again, the 1958 date here is the copyright date, not the year of manufacture. Since the body continued to be cast from the same molds for many years, the date remained the same for the life of the mold type. In 1963, the Roman numerals were changed to Arabic numerals. To date, Mattel is still using a 1966 stamp on Barbie® doll bodies.

The ability to identify the dolls' marks requires time and patience to develop, but it's essential. Once you can determine that the correct body is with the right head, you may be looking at buying a bargain. Or you will know to walk away from a completely incorrect "marriage" of parts.

Early Barbie® dolls can be identified by differences in their hair color and styling. In 1959, the Barbie® doll had a ponytail and was offered as a blonde or a brunette. A ponytailed redhead, called "titian," was introduced in 1961. The hairstyle was changed in 1962, 1963, 1964, and 1966. Learning the subtle differences among the styles will add to your ability to judge rarity and value. You may find an early body coupled with a later head (indicated by its hairstyle). This "marriage" may, in fact, be factory made, as Mattel routinely used up its inventories of parts before moving on to the new production pieces.

A surer way to tell the age of a Vintage doll is by the weight of the body. The solid-bodied dolls sold between 1959 and 1960 are heavier by one tenth of a pound, approximately .38 pound (with no clothing), versus later hollow-bodied dolls that weigh .28 pound.

Another way knowledgeable collectors can date Barbie® dolls is by the body vinyl. Over time, the early dolls from 1959 and 1960—#1, #2, and #3—take on an almost ghostly pallor from exposure to light. The #4 dolls, by contrast, have retained the original skin tone. Collectors may also notice that some dolls have an oily look, which is commonly called "greasy face." These were produced in 1961; the appearance is due to a change in vinyl formulation that year.

Rarity

Rarities occasionally come onto the market in the Barbie® doll collecting world, but much less frequently than they did in the early 1990s when values were up. The dolls that sold in that hot market have gone into collections, and relatively few are being resold. The best source for reference materials on rarities and prototype items, which are explained in detail below, are the back issues of the bimonthly magazines. Also, *The Story of Barbie®* by Kitturah B. Westenhouser contains lots of photos and is an excellent reference guide.

The #1 Ponytail Barbie® is possibly the rarest and most-sought after of dolls. After all, it was the first. Mattel had few orders on the doll and were not sure if it would sell, so they limited production to approximately 200,000 units. Many of these dolls were discarded once a child finished playing with them or were turned in during the 1967 Barbie Trade-In event, when Mattel let owners exchange old Barbie® dolls for the new Twist 'N Turn™ doll for $1.50. In May 1967, 1,250,000 Barbie® dolls were exchanged.

Also, brunettes were made in a one-to-two ratio to blonde versions and thus command a higher price. Easter Parade, one of the first outfits, is also a significant rarity. In the Contemporary market, the Limited Edition Gold Jubilee Barbie® doll, released in 1994 to celebrate the doll's thirty-fifth anniversary, sold initially for $295, with 5,000 dolls released in the U.S. market. Within weeks, the secondary market price had exceeded $1,000. What makes it so desirable? It's a gorgeous doll, and Mattel advertised it to be made of a special "porcelain vinyl."

Trade-in Twist 'N Turn™ doll

Prototypes and Variations

A *prototype* is a handmade doll or outfit that Mattel made to determine whether or not to put it into production. Then *samples* are produced for the fashion designing staff to complete the wardrobe details and patterns for clothing production.

A number of Vintage prototype dolls and outfits in the collecting world purportedly came from Mattel employees during the 1960s. Who currently has an item, what its history is and how it is

---

Limited, Collector, and Special Editions

Limited editions, as declared by Mattel, are collector dolls that are produced in limited numbers. Currently, the most that can be produced and still carry the limited edition designation is 35,000 dolls; however, many quotas are significantly below this. An example of a limited edition is the Bob Mackie series of dolls, which has been produced since the early 1990s. While the value of some of these dolls has increased significantly, others could retail on the secondary market for below their original selling price, underscoring again the importance of buying what you love, not buying as an investment. Collector edition dolls are produced in greater numbers than limited edition dolls, but their designs carry a level of detail that still makes them of special interest to collectors. A special edition doll is generally produced for a particular store or account, such as Target or Toys 'R' Us. The exception is the Happy Holidays series, which was produced for general release and was quite successful both for Mattel and for collectors. The dolls, originally retail priced between $30 and $40, are now valued at between $50 and $950.

---

documented, plus the credibility of the people involved in the chain of ownership, are all important in determining its legitimacy.

The problem with variations and prototypes is that there are no experts. You may be lucky to see a single example, either in person or in a photograph. Even the most seasoned dealers, who have undoubtedly seen a larger number of legitimate variations than most collectors, can't easily claim the depth of knowledge in this subject necessary to call themselves experts. Proceed with great caution with any interests you may have in collecting prototypes. Usually only very advanced collectors venture into this arena.

As collectors become more familiar with how clothes and dolls are made, they can more readily spot rare items and production variations, as the unusual elements will just "jump out" at them—but not always at others. For example, for many years, a Bubble Cut Barbie® doll was just that, a doll with a bubble cut. In the late 1980s, however, a collector of Bubble Cuts noticed that the rooting pattern on some seemed different. These became known as Side-Part Bubble Cut dolls, and their prices skyrocketed. While many collectors eagerly searched for Side-Part Bubble Cuts, others scoffed at the idea, regarding it as wishful thinking or worse. So be confident of, and comfortable with, purchases of variations.

A genuine variation should be worth considerably more than the usual version, but often collectors shy away from such items because of the risk that these dolls may have been tampered with. It is relatively easy for an unscrupulous person to carefully open a sealed Barbie® box, remove and redress the doll, carefully reseal the box, and claim to have a variation.

Attribution

For someone interested in a particular designer's work, obviously the name is important. Until 1985, the Barbie® doll did not have her own nationally known designer. Her gowns mirrored the fashions of the times, with designs inspired by the works of Dior, Balmain, and Balenciaga. That all changed when Oscar de le Renta designed four exclusive evening gowns for the doll that had no full-sized counterparts. Mr. De la Renta even made an appearance at the Toy Fair where these designs were first shown. In 1990, Bob Mackie created a fabulous gold-beaded gown for the doll. He designs a new Barbie® doll ensemble each year. Mr. Mackie, along with some of Mattel's designers, held a number of doll signings as these designer dolls were released. Designer-signed dolls and/or

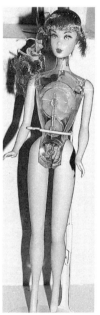

Extremely rare prototype dolls

#1 Barbie® doll in
Sheath Sensation

boxes are worth slightly more than those unsigned. In addition, Mattel's own in-house designers have developed followings among collectors.

Provenance

Provenance, in the true sense, pertains to the documented record of a doll's ownership. For example, several book authors have sold off their Barbie® doll collections at premium prices, giving the new owners bragging rights that they own such-and-such doll that was pictured "in the book." A letter transferring ownership gives purchases like this the authenticity they should have. But even documentation doesn't ensure that the next purchaser will pay a premium price for the "cachet" of its previous ownership.

Imitations, Restorations, and Reproductions

When the Barbie® doll became popular in the early 1960s, several toy companies copied it. The copies were generally made of very thin, almost see-through plastic and had molded hair. It's pretty hard to mistake these knock-offs for the real thing. The real Barbie® dolls are stamped "Mattel" on her hip, and Mattel conspicuously labels everything they manufacture. The company is also vigilant about copyright infringements and violations of its trademarks.

Quality restoration can make less-valuable dolls appear more valuable. In one example, a Color Magic Barbie® doll's hair was re-rooted to resemble a rare side-part American Girl Barbie® doll. In another, a #3 Ponytail Barbie® doll was repainted to look like a #2 Ponytail

Barbie® doll, which is a much rarer doll. It's difficult for most collectors, and even some dealers, to identify these frauds. Thus, you should be very cautious when buying rare items. Always buy from people you know and trust, and avoid any deal that looks too good to be true, because it probably is.

Mattel has made reproductions of some of their Vintage dolls. These are intentionally different enough in design from the originals to minimize confusion, and they carry different markings. The nice thing about them is that they allow collectors to have something "vintage" without paying Vintage prices.

The value of Vintage dolls has not gone down because of these reproduction dolls. Reissues of Contemporary dolls are another story, however. Mattel reissued the three rarest dolls from the International/Dolls of the World™ Collection, and even though the new dolls were completely different, the values of the original three dropped.

It really is almost impossible to spot a well-restored original doll because there are so many skilled restorers working. You must rely on the reputation of the dealer in question. If you think a doll looks suspect, ask the dealer. If the dealer says she isn't sure if the doll is legitimate or retouched, walk away from it. Why take the chance, especially with a supposedly rare, costly doll? If the dealer cannot, or will not, stand behind the legitimacy of the doll before you purchase it, you're on your own if you buy it and then later determine that the doll is less than authentic. Many dealers buy exclusively from the original owners, because it's a way to maximize the likelihood that the doll has not been altered or restored. Most original owners do not possess the skills, nor the inclination, to restore a doll, let alone to restore it well enough to avoid detection.

#1 Barbie® doll
in Nitey Negligee

GENUINE
TEEN AGE FASHION MODEL™
BY MATTEL

Barbie®

Barbie® GENUINE
TEEN AGE FASHION MODEL™
BY MATTEL

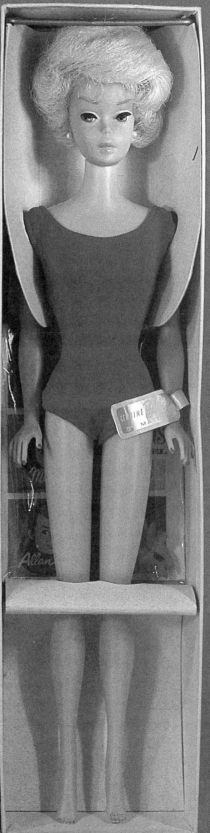

BRINGING YOUR COLLECTION INTO YOUR DAILY LIFE

For many people, part of the fun of collecting Barbie® dolls is looking at them as often as you can and posing Barbie® doll and her friends in various scenes around your home. In this section, you will learn how various collectors "live" with their Barbie® dolls. You'll get tips for displaying them in your home, learn how to take care of them, and find out how to clean and repair them if the need arises. You'll also learn how to keep track of the value of your collection, how to have it appraised, and how to insure it.

The Options for Displaying Your Barbie® Dolls

Many collectors display Barbie® dolls in their homes. Some enjoy displaying their dolls in Mattel structures. Others may use showcases. Some collectors display their dolls in a designated space in their homes. Others arrange the dolls throughout their house, making them part of the overall decorating scheme. For those who have the luxury of a spare room, dolls can be displayed on floor-to-ceiling shelves or in any manner you choose. It all depends on how many dolls you have to show off.

opposite:
1963 Bubble Cut
Barbie® doll

For those who do not have a whole room to devote to their Barbie® doll collection, curio cabinets, placed wherever space allows throughout the home, make for pleasing displays. Most experienced collectors are wary of decorating with their dolls because of risk of damage, but displaying dolls in a closed cabinet will protect them from dust and other airborne damage. You can pick up one of these cabinets at just about any furniture store, including a secondhand furniture store or even a flea market or tag sale. The ideal cabinet will have adjustable, wide shelves and glass on both front and sides to allow you to display a variety of dolls at once.

You may like to try posing your dolls in scenes—in a wedding or at a ski lodge, for example. In September, your Barbie® and Skipper® dolls can be getting ready to go back to school. In October, they might be costumed for Halloween. During the winter holidays, decorate a miniature room, complete with Christmas tree and gifts, or create an elegant ball for New Year's Eve.

Themes, like the mod 1960s and the disco era of the 1970s make fabulous displays. Do you collect Vintage dolls and outfits? If so, why not take the opportunity to step back in time and display a Barbie® doll in a poodle skirt standing next to a Ken® doll

---

Planning Your Displays

How you organize and display your collection will be as personal as the choices you make about which dolls to acquire. For inspiration, the following are some ways other collectors have organized their dolls.

- By Appearance. Many collectors like to group their dolls by the color or design of their outfits. Barbie® dolls wearing pink outfits are in one group, dolls dressed in plaids or florals in others, and so on. Another way to group the dolls is by hair color.
- By Theme. This is one of the most common ways to group Barbie® dolls. Many collectors group all Vintage dolls, all career dolls, or all casual dolls. Some may even arrange them by the age of the doll or by the purchase date.
- By Series. This is a very popular way to group Contemporary dolls. Obvious groupings are the Happy Holidays Barbie® series, The Great Eras Collection, Hollywood Legends Collection, and Hallmark-issued dolls.
- By Designer. A small segment of collectors group their dolls by clothing designer, as with the Bob Mackie and Oscar de la Renta dolls.

in his letterman's jacket? Add a miniature jukebox, and you're back in a 1950s soda shop!

Use the cardboard structures made by Mattel as backdrops or look for Barbie® doll–sized furnishings or items. The Vintage Fashion Shop, where dolls can be dressed and displayed on the runway, in the audience, or as customers in the store is a favorite for collectors. The ever-popular Vintage Little Theater is also a fun piece with a large area to stage plays. The dolls' original boxes, if you have them, may be displayed beside your dolls, but for Vintage dolls these are not generally found in great condition and may detract from your display.

Susy Goose furniture

One reason to continue changing your displays throughout the year is to protect your dolls. Dyes from the fabrics on your dolls' outfits can bleed into the vinyl. Shoes, if left on a doll for an extended period of time, may split and be ruined, or the color may stain a doll's feet.

No matter how you choose to display your collection, remember one thing: Always keep your dolls and their clothing out of direct sunlight. Set up displays away from windows. Rooms on the north side of the house, which rarely experience direct sunlight, are always better choices than rooms with other exposures. Direct sunlight can fade outfits by several shades in a matter of months and change the vinyl color of early Barbie® dolls.

The best way to display your dolls is in enclosed display cases or curio cabinets, posed standing so their outfits do not develop deep creases from being in a sitting position. Light your display with incandescent light (normal light bulbs). Steer clear of fluorescent lights because these also fade clothing. For best results, hang light-blocking shades on each window and turn on the incandescent lighting only when your dolls are being viewed.

Fashion Shop
interior

Protection and Storage

Contemporary Barbie® dolls can be a challenge to display if you've developed a large collection, because they are generally kept in their original boxes, eliminating the opportunities for creative posing and props. Contemporary dolls are often relegated to a spare bedroom or closet instead of being kept out on display.

Vintage Barbie® dolls and clothes should be kept out of the reach of small children—not to mention pets! Some dogs think that Barbie® dolls make a wonderful chew toy, while cats can derive hours of pleasure batting around those tiny Barbie® doll pumps.

Your dolls and clothing should be stored at constant room temperature—about 65 to 70 degrees—and away from temperature extremes and excessive moisture. Basements, attics, and garages are usually unsuitable for Barbie® dolls. Attics and garages can experience dramatic fluctuations in temperature if they are not properly insulated and ventilated, and basements are generally prone to mold and mildew, which can quickly ruin an entire collection.

Display and store dolls in rooms away from the kitchen to avoid odors and grease. Also, do not display your dolls and accessories in areas where people smoke. More than one collector has been frustrated by not being able to get the smell of cigarette smoke out of her dolls' hair or clothes; prolonged exposure to smoke can also discolor clothing.

Take care with the stands you use to display your dolls. The original stands may not be your best choice. The earlier ones, especially, have sharp points that may harm the outfits. Also, any metal in direct contact with clothing may leave rust or corrosion marks behind. Try the newer doll stands that are made specially for Barbie® dolls and fit around the waist. The wire on these stands is coated in plastic, which will protect the clothes. You'll find them at just about any doll show or at your local doll shop.

Store Vintage Barbie® doll fashions flat between layers of acid-free tissue paper in cardboard boxes. Be sure not to place them in direct contact with wood or cardboard, which may contain acid that can darken fabrics.

If you have to move, pack Barbie® first. Leave the outfits on the dolls if possible, and wrap acid-free tissue paper around the doll and inside the skirt. This will keep the outfit in formed shape, not creased and crushed in the packing material. For Vintage boxed dolls, wrap tissue around the doll to cradle it, then wrap more tissue around the box. Finish by wrapping the box with bubble wrap. When filling a packing carton, put heavier boxes on the bottom and then layer up with lighter ones. Never overpack a carton and risk crushing a box or a doll. Fill in any gaps with Styrofoam popcorn. For Contemporary boxed dolls, wrap the boxes first in acid-free tissue and then in bubble wrap, and do not stack them more than two boxes high in the packing carton; the plastic windows on the fronts of the Barbie® boxes may split, tear, or become detached from the inside of the box.

Long-Term Storage

If you've packed your Vintage Barbie® doll collection for a move, it's best to unpack it again as soon as you've settled into your new home and cleaned up the moving dust and dirt that might harm your dolls. If you need to keep your dolls in storage for a prolonged period, you should take some additional precautions.

Wrap outfits and dolls in acid-free paper or cotton. Do not

COLLECTOR'S COMPASS

TM

Don't let just anyone who comes knocking at your door know that you have a Barbie® doll collection. Collectible dolls are recognized to be valuable by almost everyone these days. Your conspicuously displayed Barbie® doll collection may serve as an advertisement to burglars. As with other valuables that you take care to keep from public view, it's a good idea not to display your dolls within sight of the front door or in the foyer of your home, nor in a location that's easily visible through windows from the street. Most serious collectors show their collections only to trusted friends and fellow collectors.

If someone comes to your home ostensibly to look at dolls for purchase, show them the dolls you intend to sell in an area that doesn't put your entire collection in plain sight. This is sad, but necessary advice. Because of the huge values assigned to certain Barbie® dolls and because they are fairly small, they are highly appealing to thieves.

place them in airtight food storage bags, as dolls should get some air circulation. Any moisture that's trapped in the bag will eventually damage the doll. Pack the dolls loosely in acid-free cardboard cartons. If you store your dolls and outfits in large plastic storage bins, puncture the lid in a few places to allow air to circulate and humidity to equalize. Never store either cardboard cartons or plastic bins directly on the floor. Humidity may condense under them and wick through the cardboard to reach the dolls. And in the most tragic scenario, your precious dolls stored on the floor may be the first victims of a broken water pipe or other plumbing disaster.

Care and Cleaning

Periodic maintenance of your Vintage Barbie® dolls and accessories is essential, whatever the overall condition of your collection. Many Barbie® books devote sections to restoring and caring for dolls and outfits. Read these completely and carefully before you attempt any type of cleaning procedure. Back issues of the bimonthly magazines also have lots of articles that will help. Barbie® maintenance is simple; however, damage can easily result if it's not done properly.

A light cleaning can be done by anyone, but extensive work should be left to someone with experience. And dolls that are properly cared for should require nothing more than a light wipe with a soft, dry cloth, as infrequently as possible.

It is important to try to arrest "green ear" if you see signs of it. Left untreated, the discoloration will continue to spread even after the brass earrings are removed. Try to halt the damage by applying a small amount of 10-proof hydrogen peroxide—the kind used as a disinfectant—directly to the green stain with a cotton swab. Be careful to keep the peroxide away from the doll's face paint, because it can cause fading. If the condition continues to spread after several periodic applications, seek the help of a professional doll doctor.

If you must remove obvious dirt or smudges, clean Barbie® doll faces with a tiny amount of mild soap on a slightly dampened soft cloth. Use a light hand, because the face paint may not hold up to vigorous rubbing. In addition to taking off face paint, scrubbing can allow water to easily seep into a shoulder joint or into the neck hole and possibly mildew the doll. If possible, avoid any cleaning altogether.

Repairs and Restorations

Minor clothing repairs, such as replacing missing snaps and buttons, usually can be done without adversely affecting value by just about any collector who can handle a needle and thread. Seams and hems are best left to someone who knows how to use a sewing machine well, as the tiny size of doll clothing can be challenging. Contact a professional seamstress if you are not confident with a sewing machine. An amateurish repair job will be objectionable to most collectors, and the clothing will be difficult, if not impossible, to sell.

One restoration that has been accepted by many Vintage Barbie® doll lovers is the restyling of a doll's hair to its original condition. Barbie® doll magazines usually feature articles on how to wash and restyle the hair. If your doll has had her hair trimmed by a previous owner, dress her in a hat. This will disguise the defect for your display purposes, but you must, of course, reveal the condition to a potential buyer.

Body repairs should be left to professional restoration artists. These artists generally work primarily for dealers because they can realize a consistent income from them, which makes it difficult for

When in doubt, don't fix it. Sometimes, even with green ear, it's best to leave the doll alone. There are many ways to enjoy a doll, blemishes and all. One collector we spoke to fondly remembers a beautiful-faced titian Ponytail Barbie® she had. Unfortunately, the doll's ears had turned green, and the stain ran down each side of the doll's face and onto her back. One day, the collector found a wonderful Little Theater costume called Guinevere, which had a cowl that completely covered the doll's ears and the back of her head. You'd never know the now-stunning doll was a green-ear victim!

Bubble Cut Barbie® doll in the Guinevere costume

individual collectors to pin them down. If you manage to find one, the repair might take months to complete because restorers almost always put the dealers' work first. Thus, your best bet is to go through a dealer, even though she may mark up the cost of restoration to cover her time and trouble. Or, if you're a regular customer, the dealer may put you in direct touch with the restoration artists and doll doctors she uses. Also, Barbie® doll magazines feature listings for doll doctors. Ask for and check references before you send your valuable dolls and outfits to anyone. A poor repair can be worse than no repair.

The flaws seen on a Barbie® doll are usually the result of the love a child gave her long ago. If the defects bother you, repair them. However, if you can overlook them, why not just enjoy the doll as she is? Most repairs cost more than the end result is worth anyway. Of course, you may restore a childhood doll for no other reason than sentimental value. The cost of the repair may be irrelevant because the doll is irreplaceable.

Record Keeping

As with any collectible that's been recognized to have value over time, we are all temporary "stewards" of our collections. It's our duty to keep our treasures in good stead until it's time to put them into the hands of the next caring collector.

But taking proper care of your dolls is only part of the responsibility. Keeping good records and making sure you've safeguarded your investment in them is the other side of it.

Dealer Contacts

Always get a receipt when you buy a doll. Keep a copy of any dealer's list from which you placed an order. Note your experience with the dealer—good or bad. This information will come in handy months later when you may want to place another order with that dealer.

Also, it's wise to keep in contact with dealers regularly. Dealers often trade with collectors they know, and they will often keep "want" lists on file for favorite customers. A want list for general distribution (at shows, malls, flea markets, etc.) should include your name, phone number, and e-mail address (if you have one) as well as the date the list was last compiled or edited, any special conditions or qualifications, and your general price range. Dealers often discard these lists after thirty to sixty days, so send an updated list every month or so. Don't divulge your address generally; give it only to a dealer from whom you are buying a doll. Even then, a post office box is preferable to using your street address in the collecting world. Another point of sad, but necessary advice.

Formal Inventory

You need to keep track of what you own, and the bigger your collection gets, the more important having a formal inventory becomes. For each purchase, record the date, amount paid, the dealer's name, a description of the item, identifying marks, and any other relevant notes. If you have a database software program on your computer, it's fairly easy to create a simple database to capture the required information, which you can then sort for various purposes. The form we've included on page 114 may be photocopied for your own use, but it is a violation of copyright for you to sell or distribute it to others.

Take individual photos of each item in your collection. Your insurance agent may also suggest that you do this. As with any other important documentation, your inventory and all

Welcome to My Collection

Date of purchase: _____

Purchase price: _____

Description of doll: _____

_____

_____

Conditions /defects: _____

_____

Description of outfit: _____

_____

Condition/defects: _____

_____

Accessories included: _____

_____

Accessories missing: _____

_____

Box included: _____

Condition/defects: _____

Other comments/notes: _____

_____

_____

From whom purchased: _____

Address: _____

Phone: _____

Fax: _____

E-mail: _____

Where purchased: _____

_____

photographs should be kept outside your home in a safe-deposit box, where you may already be keeping other important records. Be sure to update your inventory and photos regularly. Once a month is a good discipline if you're actively adding to your collection.

Appraisal

You may need to have your collection appraised for a number of reasons. Your insurer may require that you have an appraisal done if you intend to insure your collection, especially if you own single items with a value over a certain dollar amount. You may be thinking of donating your collection to a qualifying institution for the tax benefit it may provide you. You may need to have your collection professionally valued as part of a divorce settlement or in planning how your estate will be bequeathed to your heirs. A professional appraisal will include the reason for which the appraisal was performed; different reasons can change the method of valuation used.

An appraisal is a significant undertaking. It requires knowledge, research, sometimes consultation with other experts, and finally a thoroughly detailed, written, and certified description and valuation of everything in your collection. The appraisal should include a statement of why the appraisal was performed; complete descriptions of the items, including photos; the method of valuation used; and the market for which the collection is being evaluated.

All this stated, two things should be obvious: First, appraisals should be performed only by a fully credentialed appraiser, certified by one or more of the national appraisers' societies, and preferably a doll specialist. Second, appraisals are expensive, and you either need to have a compelling reason to have one done or be prepared for the cost of the appraisal to equal or exceed the value of your collection if you don't own some real rarities.

By the way, a reputable appraiser should never base his or her fees on a percentage of the appraised value of your collection. Nor should the appraiser express any interest in buying or auctioning your collection should you be evaluating its worth for sale. Both practices are unethical and signal that you should look elsewhere.

Dream Kitchen

The appraiser should quote either a package price or a per-hour rate.

The best way to secure an appraiser's services is by referral from a trusted collector friend or your attorney. You may want to check with your local auction houses for recommendations, too. If you have access to the Internet, visit the Web sites of the national appraisers' societies, which have state-by-state listings of their members to help you find someone qualified in your area: International Society of Appraisers (ISA) www.isa.org and the American Society of Appraisers (ASA) www.appraiser.org. If you have to resort to a phone directory, look for appraisers who are certified by one of these organizations. When you call, ask if they're doll or toy specialists.

Most appraisers require that you sign a contract for their services. The contract should include the completion date, a detailed description of the services to be rendered, total fees, and payment schedule. Be prepared to pay 50 percent on signing, with the balance due on delivery of the written appraisal report.

An appraisal is admissible as evidence in a court of law. It is also a confidential document bound by the same client-professional privilege that applies to the work of attorneys and doctors. The appraiser may not divulge the contents of his or her appraisal to anyone without the client's written permission or request.

Finding a qualified appraiser in the Barbie® doll arena is difficult. Many formal appraisals are done by certified doll appraisers who may completely misidentify a Barbie® doll. The appraiser should be personally knowledgeable about Barbie® dolls or he should use a Barbie® doll expert with valid credentials or references in this field as a consultant.

Insurance

Depending on the size and value of your collection, you may want to insure it separately from your homeowner's or renter's property insurance policy. You can attach a rider to your homeowner's policy, but this may be expensive and may be restricted to those individual items that exceed a specified dollar amount in value. Talk to your insurance agent about the menu of policy upgrades or separate policies available to you, and make sure you understand whether they cover the original value, the intrinsic value, or the replacement/market value of your dolls. Most personal-property insurance calculates that items held over time depreciate in value, when, hopefully, just the opposite is happening to the value of your Barbie® dolls.

Some insurance companies specialize in collectible insurance. These specialized policies may be less expensive than a rider to your current homeowner's or personal-property policy. You may also want to investigate whether your local Barbie® doll collectors' group offers group insurance policies to members. That in itself may justify your joining.

COLLECTOR'S COMPASS

"Appraisal" is a frequently misused term. Often doll shows advertise free appraisals, which means a dealer stationed at the front of the room will quickly examine items and verbally estimate a value. This is not a valid appraisal, nor is it a reliable way to find out the value of a doll. An appraiser in this position may be inclined to understate the value to favor dealers buying dolls at the show.

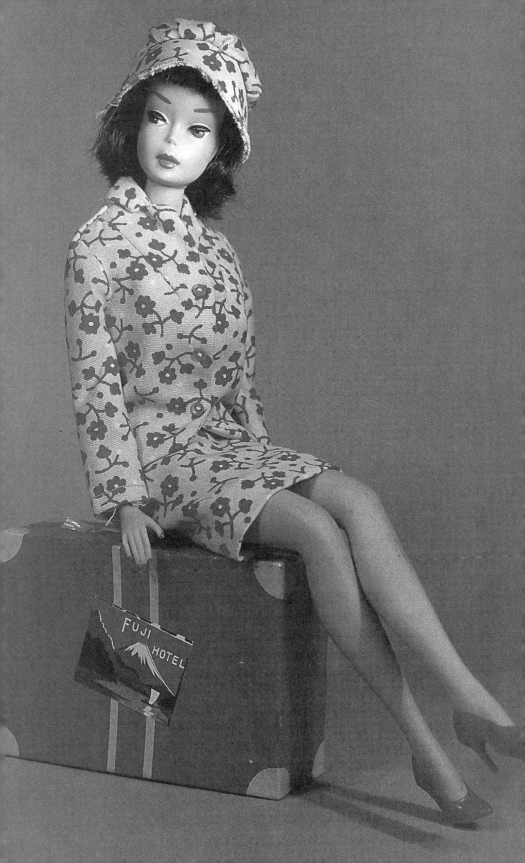

SELLING YOUR COLLECTION

From Collector to Seller

As great as your passion for Barbie® dolls may be, you may want or need to sell some or all of your dolls at some point. When you do, there are a variety of ways to go about it—some quicker than others, some more work than others, and some more likely than others to be profitable for you.

One of the most common reasons to sell is to trade up. Perhaps you've found an example in much better condition than the doll you already have. Maybe you've zeroed in on your collecting specialty, and some of the dolls you own are now outside the scope of that theme. You may have amassed duplicates in the course of buying up large lots of dolls or accesssories to get the few items you really needed. Maybe you've simply learned more about the dolls you've purchased over time, and being more knowledgeable, you're less interested in some of them now.

People's personal circumstances change. Perhaps your collecting budget is greater now than it was when you first started. Today, dolls of a much higher rarity or desirability are your game, and the more common ones you bought a few years ago don't hold as much appeal. Perhaps you're contemplating financing a major purchase

opposite:
American Girl
Barbie® doll in
Travel Togethers

An Auction That Became a Business

One enterprising collector tried putting her unwanted inventory up for auction. Her early auctions were done by mail and run from her home. Only about 50 people received the auction catalog, which was sent out about three weeks before the closing date. The format was typical of mail/phone auctions: bids could be sent by mail, phone, or fax until closing day, when bidders called in to see if they were high and bid up, if they chose, until the final bid was realized.

Over time, the number of subscribers grew, the number of auctions increased, and a live auction was held in Washington, D.C. By that time, collectors were coming from all over the country and around the world to bid on the items in person. At that point, after five years, the auction business had grown to be so successful that the founder sold it.

---

or expense—a new home, a college education, etc.—and the money you've invested in your collection needs to be freed up (if only for a time) for another purpose. Maybe you're downsizing your household, and you simply won't have the space you once enjoyed for your huge collection. Maybe your collection has just become too huge to enjoy.

You may have been collecting Contemporary Barbie® dolls all along with the hope that you'd buy well and be able to turn a nice profit on your investment at some point. If you're a speculative collector, "timing" the market to sell at its peak is a matter of close attention and luck similar to techniques used in stock trading.

Adverse circumstances—divorce, job loss, medical catastrophe, and others—can also compel you to sell. In these cases, you may need a quick solution for liquidating your collection.

Or, you may be intrigued with the experience of standing on the other side of the selling table. Avid collectors often become part-time, episodic, or even full-time dealers as a way to spend more time with the thing they love. Dealers may pluck the gems from their inventories for their personal collections, or they may simply take delight in handling more Barbie® dolls than they ever could by only collecting them for themselves. And becoming a dealer puts you in league with other sellers; suddenly you've gained entrée to a "sorority" that may provide you with even greater access to knowledge, lore, and the dolls themselves.

Whatever your reason for selling, here's where good record keeping pays off. If you have every item in your collection described in a database or even on a set of inventory forms, it will be easy for you to review what you have to sell. Being able to reference what you paid for items will help you to set your prices. If you took care to capture the details of a doll's condition, defects, and completeness of the accessories, you've already gone a long way toward writing a listing—whether for an ad, a price tag, or an online auction.

Trading Up

What do you do with pieces you've outgrown? The next time you go to a doll show, try taking a couple of your "excess" dolls along and see if you can find a dealer who will buy or trade with you. Keep in mind, a dealer might have several dolls like yours already, so she might not be motivated to give you the best deal on a sale. However, she may be willing to trade if the item you want is not one she's invested a lot of time and money in, or if she's had trouble selling it. It's largely a hit-or-miss proposition, but the worst prospect is that you'll have to take the dolls back home at the end of the day. If you have a rare item, it will probably be better for you to sell it than trade it.

Selling for the Money

Selling your collection because you need the money is not the ideal situation, but let's face it: kids need braces and college tuition has to be paid. More urgent situations like an illness, job loss, or a move may force you to sell. If you've kept good records, you should be able to liquidate fairly quickly. There are several different avenues to explore.

Sell the Entire Collection to a Dealer

This option will probably net you the lowest return on your money invested, as dealers only pay a percentage of current market value—usually 50 percent or less. They have overhead to cover and deserve to make a profit for their trouble. If you've held your dolls for a long time, even the wholesale prices a dealer will pay could give you a gain over what you originally paid. And you may be fortunate to own dolls that have become more desirable over time.

Depending on your circumstances, the speed, ease, and convenience of selling your collection as a whole may outweigh the money issue. You'll be able to take your money directly to the bank. (Speaking of this, get cash, a money order, or a certified check if you're selling to a dealer with whom you have no prior experience.) You will avoid many of the selling headaches—keeping track of individual sales, packing and shipping dolls and accessories, bad checks, disgruntled purchasers, and being stuck with items that just won't move.

Ask the dealer who's interested in buying your collection if a complete, detailed inventory is necessary before investing the time to create one. He may want to inspect your inventory in person and then determine his price. If that's the case, you're well served to have gone through your collection item by item anyway, to total up what you think it's worth and how much you're willing to take for it.

Consign Your Collection to a Dealer

You may get a greater return on your collection going this route, but it will take longer to sell it. Here, you definitely need an item-by-item inventory and a specific price for each item. You may need to discuss your price expectations with the consignee. While the dealer's going to get a percentage of the selling price as his commission, he'll be reluctant to handle an item if you have unrealistic price expectations that are going to keep the doll in his inventory for too long. Pay close attention to clarifying the details of your arrangement and get them in writing, signed by both of you.

One of the best reasons to enter into an arrangement like this is that full-time dealers cover more ground than you likely do; they may operate at shows, in malls, and even over the Internet simultaneously. They also have many more contacts than you'll have and a ready supply of want lists from other collectors who are ready to buy. The commission you pay them to get this access to their selling network is well worth it.

Sell Your Collection Yourself

This is the most time-consuming way to sell a collection, both in terms of what you'll have to put into it as well as how long it will

1960s gift set

take you to sell. Not only will you need to be on top of the market, you will also have to present your dolls for sale, establish a network of contacts who'll buy your stuff, and if you're selling by mail or online, you've got the hassles of following through on every transaction. You'll be on the other side of "customer service" issues—bad checks, complaints, tracking shipments—the whole deal.

The Internet is the most popular venue for a self-seller, but it also has its drawbacks. If you use one of the big online auctions, such as eBay, Amazon, or Yahoo!, and you make an innocent mistake or fail to hold up your end of a transaction reliably, it might lead to a posting of negative feedback that will make other buyers wary of you. If you run an ad in a Barbie® doll magazine, you'll have put out money, and there's no guarantee you'll ever make it back. Also, the lead time for placing ads in magazines and trade papers takes away precious weeks before anyone even sees your ad to contact you. With either an online auction or an ad, you're best served to include photos, which is an additional expense and time consideration.

Other considerations of Internet selling are registering to sell (which requires you to set up a credit card account with the auction to which fees will be automatically billed), the listing fee (which is minor, considering that you should be realizing "retail" selling prices), and the time it takes to write a good description. In fact, whether you're selling through an ad or on the Internet, your description can make or break your sale. Also, make sure you list your auctions in the proper category. Otherwise, someone looking for a specific item may never find it.

Another drawback of advertisements and Internet selling, compared with a show, is that you have to wait for your money. And do wait for the money! You should specify in your ads and listings that personal checks will be held until they clear; purchases paid with a money order will be shipped immediately. PayPal, BillPoint, or some other credit card payment service will allow immediate risk-free payment to you, but you'll have to set up an account with one and mention in your ads and listings that you use it.

In a worst-case scenario, you might be stuck by a high bidder who backs out of the purchase. Your only recourse is to post negative feedback. You'll then have to relist the item, which involves getting a credit for the commission on your original sale and paying a commission when the doll sells the second time around.

On the plus side, you're putting your offerings before a wide audience—wider than an individual dealer can deliver. And if you have any rarities or highly desirable dolls to auction, it only takes two people desperate to add a particular doll to their collections to drive the bidding up beyond what you could hope to realize from most other sources.

Becoming a Dealer

Many collectors who have acquired a lot of stuff eventually find themselves considering this role. And why not? What better way is there to make an income than by dabbling in something you're passionate about?

But being a dealer is not as easy as printing business cards and renting a table or booth at a show. There are many considerations, including accumulating and storing inventory, tagging each item, making arrangements for shows (reserving booth space, accommodations, travel, etc.), signing leases for space if you're trying a mall venue, writing and placing ads—not to mention your legal

The All-Important Description

An honest, complete description and photographs in good focus are essential to a successful sale, whether in a published ad or an Internet auction. Interested buyers scan a great many ads and click through long lists of page views quickly. If your description doesn't catch their eye, or if it leaves them with obvious questions unanswered, they're likely to move on. Or, you may be barraged with phone calls and e-mail questions you'll have to answer on just one item. You can waste a lot of time answering queries when you could have spent just a little more time composing your ad/listing copy. Also, if the description does not match the item as advertised, the purchaser will quite correctly demand a refund of both the purchase price and any postage and insurance that she paid. Here's a comparative example:

Poor: Early Barbie® Doll

Barbie® doll, think it is a #4 or #5 ponytail, but not sure. Light color hair, face paint looks good. Overall nice doll.

Strong: Vintage #4 Ponytail Barbie® All Original, Complete

#4 blonde Ponytail Barbie® doll includes original black-and-white striped swimsuit, pearl stud earrings, black open-toe mule shoes, white plastic sunglasses, and pink Barbie® and Ken® booklet. Doll has one extra earring hole on left ear, missing the tip of the right pinkie finger, hair in original ponytail wrap with hard curl on the end. Slight fading to end of the right eyebrow, otherwise face paint perfect, and no green staining on ears. Overall near-mint condition.

Before you start posting dolls for sale on the Internet, it's a good idea to do some online research. Search completed auctions for comparable dolls to see the kinds of prices they're fetching. See how they're described (most of the time photos are removed from completed auctions shortly thereafter). You may choose to set a reserve price, which is the lowest bid that you'll accept, especially on a doll that you know has a certain value. Check the auction rules for additional commissions that may apply on reserve price auctions.

obligations to state and federal taxing authorities. You also need to be confident that you know enough about Barbie® dolls to go into the marketplace and hold your own with other dealers as well as talk to prospective customers who will be full of questions.

Read an introductory book about running a small business or consult with a small-business counselor before you decide you want to take this route. Being a dealer is a huge investment of time—and money. Make sure you want to do this badly enough before you get in too deep. If you decide to give it a try, there are a number of ways you can go.

Shows

As a collector, you'll probably already know which are the best shows in your area in terms of the number and quality of dealers as well as crowd turnouts. But as a dealer, be prepared for an arduous experience. First, there's the red tape of renting table or booth space (which may be difficult for newcomers to obtain or may be in undesirable locations). You have to pack and transport your inventory to the show site. Then there's the "load-in" and setup, which is usually either the day before the show or at the crack of dawn the day of the show.

Be prepared for physical labor, long hours, and substantial cash outlay before your first customer even steps into your booth. Then once the show gets started—if it's a good show—you'll be standing and talking for seemingly endless hours until closing. You'll have to watch for "light-fingered" customers who may make off with your dolls. Unless you're sharing booth duties with another dealer or a buddy, you may not be able to duck away to visit the restroom or grab a quick bite when you feel like it. And when the show ends, the work of breakdown and "load-out" is still ahead.

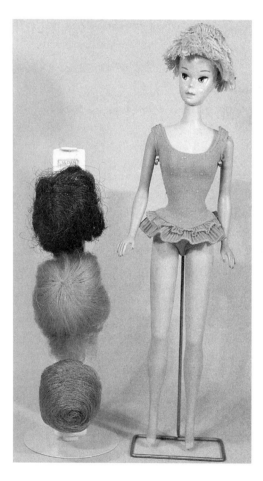

1964 Miss Barbie® doll

Of course, there are no guarantees. The show may be poorly attended for any number of reasons. If you haven't made the effort to present your inventory in an attractive way—nicely arranged and well-lit—potential customers may pass you by in favor of better merchandised booths where the dolls look fresher. Maybe your asking prices are off current market values, or other dealers show up with more desirable merchandise. Perhaps you just have a lousy spot in the back of the room. Any and all of these factors can affect your outcome.

Is it worth it? If you end up with a profit after you've covered your investment in dolls and all expenses door to door, consider it a great show. Then all the fringe benefits of hotel room hopping, buying and selling with other dealers before opening, learning more about Barbie® dolls than you knew before, and making new contacts become dividends to offset all the personal time and hard work you put into the show.

Rare cardboard store display for Fashion Queen

Malls

Antiques and collectibles malls present a number of advantages to doll sellers. They're a kind of "long-term show" in that the people who come through their doors are largely dealers and collectors, who may be looking for specific wants or just browsing. At any given moment, the traffic isn't as bustling as at a weekend show, but you capture a lot of potentially interested "eyeballs" by displaying your dolls at a mall. Depending on the mall, you may be obliged only to pay the rental fee for your space or display case plus a commission on sales. Some malls expect you to put in time there as part of your contract.

Malls are usually fairly well organized, clean, and have standard credit and discount policies. The mall employees show the items to interested customers, process credit card payments, write receipts, and wrap the purchases. You just pay the rental fee and a commission on what sells. You may also be expected to rotate your stock periodically to keep the mall's inventory looking fresh.

What could be the downside? Your merchandise can get lost among the hundreds of cases in a large mall. Malls offer general collectible merchandise, so the number of doll collectors and the number of Barbie® doll collectors coming through the door may be relatively few compared with more targeted venues.

You may find that you've associated yourself with a mall that lacks upstanding policies on carrying reproductions and fakes. While your dolls are genuine, word's out among customers to stay away from the mall. It pays to do a careful walk of the mall before committing to a lease so you can make your own observations about the overall quality of the merchandise.

In a worst-case scenario, you may find at the end of your mall lease that you sold little or nothing. In the meantime, your investment in dolls has been sitting there. That's why seasoned dealers use different sales venues simultaneously. They may be attending shows, stocking a mall case, selling online, or even putting up dolls at live auction—all simultaneously.

Live Auctions

This avenue is a lot different from online auctions, in that you're putting your dolls in the hands of a professional auctioneer. Auctions are sometimes held in association with club shows, too. In those cases, one of the club officers may act as the auctioneer.

Your concerns beforehand are:

- Is the auctioneer reputable? Auctioneers should be a member of a recognized auctioneers' association.

- Where does he advertise, and how effectively? The results of a live auction depend entirely on the turnout of bidders. You want a large crowd on auction day, but more importantly, you want individuals there who will bid on your dolls.

- Does the auctioneer produce a catalog? High-end auctions are generally cataloged. Each lot is photographed, described in detail, and perhaps given an estimate. Auctioneers who produce catalogs likely have extensive mailing lists to solicit interested collectors. The catalog may be sold individually to the public, mailed to subscribers, and/or mailed free to preferred customers.

- How will the dolls be sold? Depending on what you have to sell, you may want the most desirable dolls to be sold individually, and some of the more common ones to be included in lots of multiple dolls. The auctioneer's job is to hammer down every lot that goes on the block. If he's not a doll expert, you need to give him guidance on how dolls should be grouped or sold individually. You should also specify any reserve (minimum) prices you may want to set, though auctioneers are often resistant to reserves and would rather open the bidding at a higher level.

- What's the commission? Auctioneers usually charge a percentage on the amount of the winning bid. If you have a large collection to auction, you may be able to negotiate the commission. It never hurts to ask.

Advertising and Mail-Order Selling

You may want to try placing ads in the Barbie® doll magazines or collectibles trade papers. Your descriptive listing will be all-important (see page 109), as this is generally a two-step selling process. It's also a good idea to maintain your privacy by listing only your name, a post office box address, phone number, and e-mail address in your ads. If they work, the ads will generate correspondence from people wanting to know more. Then, you've got to be ready to send them a more detailed description and photo (a digital image if you're using the Internet) of the doll(s) in which they're interested. You may hear back from some of them a second time, with more questions or to start negotiating a purchase with you.

If you're selling Barbie® dolls on the side, mail order can be a pretty distracting way to do business. You'll get phone calls and voice-mail messages at all times of the day and night, and you'll end up playing a lot of phone tag. You have a lot of work to do, both on the phone and at the post office, to get information to people and to ship the dolls you sell. And if you're lucky and get two people interested in buying the same doll, you're faced with conducting an "auction" yourself that can easily backfire and end up in no sale.

Or, you may wonder why you're getting no calls only to learn that you missed the ad deadline and you have to sit it out for another two months. Maybe your ad didn't get good placement in the magazine and you get few calls. Most dealers who have success in this venue advertise repeatedly and set themselves up to make this a primary business.

Paying Your Taxes

If you've been a little lax about record keeping as a collector, you can't afford to make the same mistake as a dealer—whether you're selling by mail order, online, at shows, or in malls. As a seller of any kind, you're now dealing with state and federal taxing authorities.

Any state that imposes a sales tax will expect you to collect and pay state sales tax for any sales you make in person in that state. Your home state will expect you to collect and pay state sales tax on all sales you make to customers within the state—whether indirectly via mail order and the Internet or directly in person. So, if you travel to another state to do a show, be prepared to register with that state's taxing authority. Some states are more vigilant than others; it's not unusual to find state agents walking shows, randomly interviewing dealers for compliance. The show promoter will usually provide necessary information on state sales-tax compliance with your exhibitor contract and materials.

The Internal Revenue Service views your doll selling as a business activity, however casually you may do it. Get into the habit of keeping a notebook and record your expenses on every type of sale you make, from door to door—even down to the mileage when you go to the antiques mall to change the stock in your case. If you do a number of shows, you might want to get some manila clasp envelopes for receipts. Label and date one for each show you do, and stuff all your receipts into it as you go.

If you haven't kept a good inventory list or database of your dolls before now, it's essential that you make one before you start selling. Your inventory should include—at the least—a description of each doll, the documented price you paid for it, and the year in which you purchased it. The IRS is interested in any profit you recognize when you sell it over what you originally paid for the doll plus the expenses of marketing it. Your cost in the doll, in addition to your other dealer expenses, is part of the cost of selling it. If you paid to have it repaired or restored, you should have a receipt for that cost, too.

It's best to consult with your tax professional or accountant before you set out as a dealer. He or she will be able to counsel you on the details of your individual situation so that you'll be complying with the law. Your numbers person may be able to give you some pointers to help minimize the amount of tax you'll owe at the end of the year. He or she can also help you apply for a tax identification or resale number and explain why that may a good idea for you.

Donating Your Collection

You may have reasons to donate your collection to an organization or institution. Depending on your situation, it may be financially your best move, or at least one with tax advantages. Consult with your tax professional and attorney if you're considering this option and be sure you understand all the angles.

Donating your collection is a way to ensure that your dolls stay together and will be well cared for after your stewardship. First, you need to identify the institution. It may be a local museum, a library, a historical society, or other qualified nonprofit, tax-exempt organization.

Make sure the institution wants the collection, is prepared to care for it, and has a plan to exhibit it (at least initially). Work out all the details in writing before you make a commitment—what credit you'll receive, how the collection will be conserved and displayed, and whether it can ever be sold.

You may have to get the collection appraised if you're expecting a tax deduction, and, of course, your gift must be to a qualified nonprofit entity. Your tax professional will be able to guide you through the tax-compliance details relating to gifts of property.

Most importantly, make sure you're emotionally ready to part with your collection. You can visit your former collection in its new home, but once donated, you can't take your dolls back.

1964 Ponytail in Mood for Music

RESOURCES

Shows

All-Barbie® doll shows are held in major cities throughout the year. Barbie® doll items can also be found at general doll and toy shows. Check *Barbie® Bazaar* and *Miller's Fashion Doll* magazines for state-by-state listings of upcoming shows. Check your local newspaper for advertisements of general doll and toy shows in your area.

Joe Blitman and Marl Davidson take their shows all over the country, including Ft. Lauderdale, Las Vegas, Houston, Chicago, Atlanta, and New York City. For information and schedules, contact:

Joe's
　5163 Franklin Avenue
　Los Angeles, CA 90027
　Phone: 323-953-6490
　Fax 323-953-0888

Marl & B
　10301 Braden Run
　Braden, FL 34202
　Phone: 941-751-6275
　Fax: 941-751-5463
　E-mail: marlbe@aol.com
　Web site: http://auntie.com/marl

opposite:
#2 Barbie®
doll in
Suburban
Shopper

Other shows worth checking out:

Barbara Peterson's Show and Sale

This large Barbie® doll show is held in Norwalk, California, usually in January, February, March, May, and June. For information, contact:

Barbara Peterson
PO Box 5329
Fullerton, CA 92838-0329
Phone: 714-525-8420
Fax: 714-441-1701

Kitty's Collectibles & Golden Girl Productions

This show is featured in Phoenix, Austin, Denver, and Minneapolis. For information, call 602-943-2341.

Specialist Dealers

Barbara Peterson
PO Box 5329
Fullerton, CA 92838-0329
Phone: 714-525-8420
Fax: 714-441-1701
Specializes in fine Vintage Barbie® dolls and accessories.

Bits 'N Pieces Lady
Linda Holt
1141 Belfair Drive
Pinole, CA 94564
Phone: 510-924-1855
Fax: 510-724-4143
E-mail: PiecesLady@aol.com
Specializes in individual Vintage pieces to complete outfits and doll accessories. Sells at shows and has mail-order list.

Forty, Fifty, Sixty
Ben Cassara & Joe Bucchi
110 West 25th Street, 4th Floor
New York, NY 10001
Phone: 212-463-0980
E-mail: bj4t5t6t@bellatlantic.net
Specializes in vintage Barbie® items and other early toys. Shop located in New York City, but sells at local shows and online.

Joe's
5163 Franklin Avenue
Los Angeles, CA 90027
Phone: 323-953-6490
Fax: 323-953-0888
Specializes in Vintage and new Barbie® dolls. Promotes national shows and has extensive mail-order list.

Kitty's Collectibles
Scottsdale, AZ
Phone: 480-607-0421
Fax: 480-607-3317
Web site: www.kittyscol.com

Living Doll
Shelley Cole
Phone: 718-979-2829
Fax: 718-979-0658
E-mail: livdolls@aol.com

Marl & B
10301 Braden Run
Braden, FL 34202
Phone: 941-751-6275
Fax: 941-751-5463
E-mail: marlbe@aol.com
Web site: http://auntie.com/marl
Specializes in Vintage and new Barbie®
dolls. Promotes national shows and
has extensive mail-order/Web site list.

Sandi Holder's Doll Attic
2491 Regal Drive
Union City, CA 94587
Phone: 510-489-0221
Fax: 510-489-7467
Specializes in Vintage and new. Has exten-
sive mail-order list.

Auction Houses and Auctions

The following listings are for general doll and specialty Barbie®
doll auctions.

McMaster's Doll Auctions
PO Box 1755
Cambridge, OH 43725
Phone: 740-432-4419
Fax: 740-432-3191
Currently schedules two specialized Barbie® doll auctions a year.

Theirault's, The Doll Masters
PO Box 151
Annapolis, MD 21401
Phone: 301-224-3655
Fax: 301-224-2515

1998 Portland Trail
Blazers Barbie®
doll

Trade Papers and Magazines

Barbie® Bazaar **Magazine**
5617 Sixth Avenue
Kenosha, WI 53140
Phone: 414-658-1004

Doll Reader
Hobby House Press
900 Frederick Street
Cumberland, MD 21502
Phone: 717-657-9555
Fax: 717-657-9526
E-mail: www.dollreader@palmcoastd.com

Dolls **Magazine**
170 5th Avenue, 12th Floor
New York, NY 10010
Phone: 212-989-8700
Fax: 212-645-8976
E-mail: www.dollsmagazine.com

Miller's Fashion Doll **Magazine**
PO Box 8488
Spokane, WA 99203-0488
Phone: 509-747-0139
Fax: 509-455-6115
E-mail: mpublishing@uswest.net
Web site: www.millersfashiondoll.com

Clubs and Collecting Associations

Mattel has a national Barbie® doll club. Visit the official Web site for information: www.barbie.com

There are also hundreds of local Barbie® doll clubs. Refer to *Miller's Price Guide Pocket Annual* and *Barbie® Bazaar's Annual Complete Guide to Valuing Barbie® Dolls and Collectible Items.* Each of these features pages of club listings. Below are just a few:

AOLLA (Vintage club)
Los Angeles
E-mail: AnnetteMG@aol.com

The Fashion Doll Club of Eastern Oklahoma
Tulsa, Oklahoma
President: Sarah Locker
E-mail: sarah@alphabetsoup.net

Flower City Fashion Doll Club
New York
President: Carmela Gallinat
Phone: 716-223-9564

Online Auctions and Marketers

For online auctions, eBay.com and Amazon.com are sites to frequent, with periodic checks to fairmarketplace.com. and collector.com. Do keyword searches with your preferred search engine regularly as well, because smaller auctions may have moved or been discontinued, and new sites will continually crop up.

Internet collecting sites are a favorite of many Barbie® collectors. These have been listed in several publications. Following are some favorites:

www.geocities.com/Tokyo/Bay/9675
www.srhein.simplenet.com
www.dolluniverse.com
www.flash.net
www.cyberstreet.com/users/coogan/coogcoll.htm

America On-Line (AOL), Prodigy, and Compuserve all have special interest Barbie® doll groups.

RECOMMENDED BOOKS

Ten years ago, there were only two Barbie® doll reference books on the market. Then a wonderful book on just the clothing came into print. Then a book on the Francie doll was published. Now, there are more than twenty books on different phases of Barbie® doll collecting, including structures, clothing, and friends.

Barbie® Doll and Her Mod, Mod, Mod, Mod World of Fashion 1967–1972
   By Joe Blitman
   Hobby House Press, Grantsville, Maryland
   Published 1996
Barbie® Doll Exclusively for Timeless Creations: Identification and Values, Book 3
   By Margo Rana
   Hobby House Press, Grantsville, Maryland
   Published 1997
Barbie® Doll Fashion, Volume II, 1968–1974
   By Sarah Sink Eames
   Collector Books, Paducah, Kentucky
   Published 1997
Barbie® Exclusives, Book II: Identification and Values
   By Margo Rana
   Collector Books, Paducah, Kentucky
   Published 1996
Barbie® Exclusives: Identification and Values Featuring Department Store Specials, Porcelain Treasures and Disney
   By Margo Rana
   Collector Books, Paducah, Kentucky
   Published 1995
Barbie® Fashions, Volume 1, 1959–1967
   By Sarah Sink Eames
   Collector Books, Paducah, Kentucky
   Published 1990, values updated 1995
The Collectors Encyclopedia of Barbie® Dolls and Collectibles
   By Sibyl DeWein and Joan Ashabraner
   Collector Books, Paducah, Kentucky
   Published 1977, values updated 1990
Doll Fashion Anthology and Price Guide, 6th Edition
   By A. Glenn Mandeville
   Hobby House Press, Grantsville, Maryland
   Published 1998

The Story of Barbie, 2nd Edition
  By Kitturah B. Westenhouser
  Collector Books, Paducah, Kentucky
  Published 1999
The Ultimate Barbie® Doll Book
  By Marcie Melillo
  Krause Publications, Iola, Wisconsin
  Published 1996

Wedding Party gift set. Courtesy of Rosalie Whyel Museum of Doll Art. Photo by Charles Backus

ABOUT THE INTERNATIONAL SOCIETY
OF APPRAISERS

The *Collector's Compass*™ series is endorsed by the International Society of Appraisers, one of North America's leading nonprofit associations of professionally educated and certified personal property appraisers. Members of the ISA include many of the industry's most respected independent appraisers, auctioneers, and dealers. ISA appraisers specialize in over 200 areas of expertise in four main specialty pathways: antiques and residential contents, fine art, gems and jewelry, and machinery and equipment.

Established in 1979 and comprised of over 1,375 members, the ISA is founded on two core principles: to educate its members through a wide range of continuing education and training opportunities, and to promote and maintain the highest ethical and professional standards in the field of appraisals.

Education through the ISA

The cornerstone of the ISA lies in the education and accreditation programs made available to its members. In conjunction with the University of Maryland University College, the ISA offers a series of post-secondary professional courses in appraisal studies, including a two-level certification program. These programs—the first of their kind—fill a long-standing need for acknowledgment of the professional status of personal property appraisers.

The ISA recognizes three membership levels within its organization—Associate Member, Accredited Member, and Certified Member—with educational programs in place for achieving higher distinctions within the society. ISA members who complete the required coursework are recognized with the professional title of Certified Appraiser of Personal Property (CAPP). Through its pioneering educational programs, the ISA plays a vital role in producing qualified appraisers with a professional education in appraisal theory, principles, procedures, ethics, and law as it pertains to personal property appraisal.

Professional Standards of the ISA

The ISA is dedicated to the highest ethical standards of conduct, ensuring public confidence in the ability and qualifications of its members. To help members perform their work with the most up-to-date knowledge of professional standards, the ISA is continually updating, expanding, and improving its courses and criteria of conduct.

The ISA is proud to serve the public by ensuring the utmost accuracy, competency, and integrity of its members, and through setting the standards by which the profession of personal property appraising is judged.

For more information about the International Society of Appraisers, contact their corporate offices at:

Toll-free: 1-800-472-4732
E-mail: ISAHQ@isa-appraisers.org
Web: www.isa-appraisers.org

ABOUT THE CONTRIBUTORS

Chloe Hill loves vintage toys, Barbie® and family dolls in particular. Eighteen years ago, she was hooked after reading a book on old toys, and began a never-ending search for her favorite doll. Ms. Hill combs doll shows, flea markets, antique malls, and the like in her quest to find anything related to Barbie® doll. Her spare time is spent reading about Barbie® dolls, and little else. After all, the subject spans four decades and thousands of dolls, so there is much to learn. It has been a busy eighteen years, and her determination to know everything about her favorite subject has brought her to expert status in the hobby.

Irene Davis has been a collector for many years. While still in high school she attended auctions and refinished an oak hall rack from her grandmother's attic. For her graduation present in 1969, she got a "Gone With the Wind" lamp. Since then she has grown to love all types of antiques and collectibles, from formal furniture to Coca Cola and paint advertising.

When she saw a Barbie® doll–price guide about ten years ago, she pulled out her childhood dolls and started collecting. Realizing that collectors needed a way to buy items other than from list, she started the first Barbie® doll–mail auction as a part-time business. She later added a public auction that drew collectors from all over the world. She no longer collects Barbie® dolls but enjoys reading Barbie® doll magazines, looking for related items at antique shops, and helping new Barbie® doll collectors. For Irene, the love of Barbie® doll never changes.

Christopher J. Kuppig has spent his entire career in book publishing. For several years he directed programs at Dell Publishing, Consumer Reports Books, and most recently Chilton Book Company—where his assignment included managing the Wallace-Homestead and Warman's lines of antiques and collectibles guides.

In 1997, Mr. Kuppig founded Stone Studio Publishing Services, a general management consultancy to book publishers. Acting as Series Editor for the Collector's Compass has given him the opportunity to draw upon his wide-ranging network of contacts in the collecting field.

Mr. Kuppig resides with his wife and three children in eastern Massachusetts.

Gayle Christie, who contributed many of the photographs for this book, started collecting Barbie® dolls in 1984. She soon amassed a large collection and in 1986 opened a Barbie® doll museum in Grand Ronde, Oregon (the museum no longer exists). In addition to the museum, Ms. Christie's interest in Barbie® dolls also led to her writing a monthly column titled "Barbie® Talk" for *The Northwest Doll and Teddy Bear Collector* for five years and several articles for *Barbie® Bazaar*.

Although she no longer collects Barbie® dolls, she still contributes articles to various publications and continues to enjoy and research dolls as a full-time staff member for The Rosalie Whyel Museum of Doll Art in Bellevue, Washington.

INDEX

Photos appear on the page numbers listed in italics.

Harley-
Davidson®
Barbie® #3
and Ken® #1
dolls